We Don't Speak Great Things—We Live Them!

A Modern English Rendition of

Mark Felix's *Octavius*

from the translation of Robert Ernest Wallis, Ph.D.

and

The First Apology of Justin Martyr

From the translation of Marcus Dods, D.D.

SCROLL
PUBLISHING

ISBN: 092-4722-010

Library of Congress Catalog No. 89-062523
Cover illustration: © Robyn Miller, 1989
Cover design: Robyn Miller

Printed in the United States of America

To Andre and Heather,
may you always live great things.

Contents

About This Translation

Next to the Bible, the writings of the early Christians (90-325 A.D.) are the most valuable documents of Christianity. Like the Bible, they are part of the heritage of all Christians. Although these writings are not inspired, Scroll Publishing Co. believes that any translation of them should be done as carefully as that of the Scriptures.

To that end, our contemporary renditions have been taken from the scholarly, careful translations that comprise *The Ante-Nicene Christian Library*. These translations were first published in 1867, in Edinburgh, Scotland, under the editorial supervision of Alexander Roberts, D.D., and James Donaldson, LL.D. As expressed by those editors, their objective was "to place the English reader as nearly as possible on a footing of equality with those who are able to read the original. With this view they [the translators] have for the most part leaned towards literal exactness; and wherever any consider-able departure from this has been made, a verbatim rendering has been given at the foot of the page" (from the Preface to *The Ante-Nicene Christian Library*).

It was precisely this "literal exactness" that persuaded us to use *The Ante-Nicene Christian Library* translations as the basis for this work. We see little value in publishing a version of the early Christian writings that has been colored by the interpretations and theological biases of the translator. On the other hand, although we applaud the "literal exactness" of the *Ante-Nicene* translations, we realize that their stilted, archaic language discourages the modern layperson from reading them.

Therefore, the goal of Scroll Publishing is to render the early Christian works into contemporary, readable English while preserving the meaning of the original writers. To this end, we have followed a two-tiered system in our renditions:

We have been very strict in rendering passages containing material of theological, ecclesiastical, or moral significance to the modern reader. In such passages, we have aimed at "literal exact-ness," concentrating on faithfully communicating the writer's ac-tual words or phraseology. We have not deleted any material from such passages.

However, we have paraphrased those passages that do *not* contain anything of theological, ecclesiastical, or moral significance to the modern reader. In such passages, we have concentrated on capturing as exactly as possible the meaning of the original writer, using simpler, more contemporary language. In such non-doctrinal passages, we have sometimes deleted sentences that are repetitious or whose meaning is obscure. And we have deleted paragraphs that contain only tedious or repetitious information, such as descriptions of the pagan gods or philosophers. However, *all* deleted material has been reprinted in the appendices at the back of the book. Appendix One contains material deleted from *Octavius*, and Appendix Two contains material deleted from Justin's *First Apology*. Including the material in the appendices, this edition contains all of the original texts.

Our rendition of *Octavius* has been taken from the translation made by Dr. Robert Ernest Wallis for *The Ante-Nicene Christian Library*. Dr. Wallis was the "Senior Priest-Vicar" of Wells Cathedral in Somerset, England. *Octavius* is a highly polished, well organized work. Other than abridgement, the only textual change we have made was, for dramatic effect, to move the material from chapter 13 (as numbered in Dr. Wallis' translation) and include it as part of chapter 2 here.

Our rendition of Justin Martyr's *First Apology* is from the translation made by Marcus Dods, D.D., for *The Ante-Nicene Christian Library*. Dr. Dods was an ordained Presbyterian minister and Professor of New Testament Exegesis at Free Church College in Edinburgh, Scotland. Rendering Justin's *Apology* into a readable format was considerably more challenging than that of *Octavius*. As is typical of Eastern writers, Justin is more concerned with *what* he says than with the orderly flow of his ideas. As a result, he frequently digresses from one topic to another. In the end, he always returns to his original chain of thought. But in the process, he often loses his twentieth century Western reader.

Therefore, to make Justin's *Apology* more readable, we have rearranged the order of his paragraphs to follow a logical sequence. However, we have not changed the *contents* of his paragraphs. Appendix Two provides a schedule showing the rearrangement of Justin's paragraphs as numbered in the translation of Dr. Dods.

To enhance the flow of both of these works, the modern editor has occasionally added transitional sentences between chapters. Such sentences, which do not appear in the original text, are designated with a printer's cross.† The modern editor has also furnished all chapter titles, subheadings, footnotes, and Scripture citations. There were no citations in the original texts because the

Scriptures had not yet been divided into chapters and verses when these works were written.

As you read, you will come across some names that are probably unfamiliar to you. To assist you, we have included a brief biographical glossary in the back of the book. It contains a pronunciation guide and a brief biographical capsule for all proper names appearing in the main body of the text, except for names of Biblical persons.

The primary editor of this edition has been David W. Bercot. He obtained his Bachelor of Arts degree summa cum laude from Stephen F. Austin University and his Doctor of Jurisprudence degree cum laude from Baylor University School of Law. The early Christian writings have been his special field of study for a number of years. He is the author of the book, *Will The Real Heretics Please Stand Up*, which concerns the early Christians. He has also written various articles about the early church.

He was ably assisted in his work by Jeleta Eckheart, an accomplished journalist who has edited several Christian books and periodicals. She obtained her Bachelor of Arts degree in literature and journalism with highest honors from George Washington University.

A Window In Time

Do works play any role in salvation? How can a person be born again? How often should Christians celebrate communion? Is abortion a form of murder? Should baptism be by immersion or sprinkling? Is it right for a Christian to go to war?

Christians have argued about questions such as these for centuries. Even though various Christians have answered these questions differently, they have all quoted from the same Bible in support of their positions. The problem is that even though the Bible is the inspired Word of God, some Bible passages aren't clear. In fact, some verses seem to contradict other verses. Because of these uncertainties, Christians have splintered into hundreds of different sects and denominations. And they eventually turn to other sources of authority to clarify the Bible: church publications, Bible commentaries, creeds, and the instruction of pastors or seminary professors.

But how valuable are these additional sources of authority? What basis do we have for saying that our church publications are right and someone else's are wrong? How can we say that our seminary professors know more than those of another seminary? How does a seventeenth century Bible commentator like Matthew Henry know what Jesus and the apostles *really* meant? Isn't there some other source of authority closer to the New Testament? Fortunately for us, there is: the writings of the early Christians. Their writings do not claim to be inspired. They are simply an honest record of what Christians believed and practiced in the centuries immediately following the deaths of the apostles. They are our closest written link to the New Testament, and they provide us with a window in time so that we can know what Christianity was like at the close of the apostolic age.

Strangely, as important as these writings are, very few Christians have ever read them. In fact, most Christians have never even *heard* of these early Christian writers. Few church libraries have these books, and most Christian bookstores do not carry them.

Actually, it wasn't until the nineteenth century that most of the early Christian writings were published in English. Unfortunately, most of the English translations of these works were made for an academic audience. Although these translations are very sound scholastically, few Christian laypeople are willing to wade through them. As a result, the early Christian writings have remained almost exclusively the province of the academic community. Scroll Publishing believes that every Christian today should be familiar with the writings of the early Christians. Our vision is to render most of the early Christian works into modern, readable English while preserving the meaning of the original writers.

This volume contains two important early Christian apologetic works: Mark Felix's *Octavius* and Justin Martyr's *First Apology*. In literature, an apology is a formal, written defense of something. It's not an admission of fault or an expression of regret. The early Christian apologists defended Christianity and explained to the Romans and Jews what Christians actually believed and practiced. The *First Apology* of Justin Martyr is the oldest Christian apology still in existence. *Octavius*, which was written a few decades later, is arguably the *finest* early Christian apologetic work.

We can think of no better writings to introduce the modern reader to early Christianity. Not only are these two works easy to read, but they are also highly representative of early orthodox Christian thought. The answers you will find in these works to the questions posed at the beginning of this book are generally the same answers you will find in all the early Christian works. As you read *Octavius* and Justin's *Apology*, you will probably be reassured that the early Christians believed many of the same things you do. At the same time, you will undoubtedly notice some views and practices that are different from your own. That is virtually everyone's experience upon reading these writings for the first time.

Please don't become defensive about these differences. There's no Christian denomination today that believes and practices its faith in exactly the same way the second century Christians did. Instead of becoming defensive, please read these works with an honest and open heart. You may not want to change any of your views based on what you read, but hopefully you will be more tolerant of the beliefs of other Christians—particularly where their views are closer to those of the early church.

Of course, these two works by themselves do not describe all details of early Christian life nor do they discuss all of the doctrinal views of the early church. But they do provide a vivid picture of the dynamic, living church of the second century. I hope these works will enlighten you and challenge you as they have so many others.

Part One

Octavius

By Mark Felix

_____

Mark Felix: Lawyer For God

As the golden autumn sun shimmers across the deep blue waters of the Mediterranean, three men climb onto the massive wave-swept rocks that jut into the sea. They are not seeking adventure; they are searching for a secluded spot to discuss the profound questions of life: How did man get here? Is there a God? If there is a God, can we know him personally? Are our lives controlled by fate? Is there life after death? The men also talk about a fast-growing sect called the "Christians" and their novel teachings that are sweeping the Roman Empire. It's rumored that the Christians meet in secret to eat human flesh and to revel in incestuous orgies. Some say they worship a criminal who was impaled on a cross. Others say they worship a donkey's head.

Whoever they are, the Christians are certainly one of the strangest cults in the Empire. They have no temples, no altars, and no images. They take no interest in the sporting events and theaters of the day. Their religion seems to bring them only poverty and suffering.

The narrator of this discussion is Mark Minucius Felix. He is a Roman lawyer and a Christian. Caecilius (sigh SILL ee us), who is either a trusted employee or a relative of Mark, is a non-believer. When Caecilius throws a kiss to a stone image, it prompts a heated debate about Christianity between Caecilius and Mark's closest friend, Octavius. A devout Christian and a man of considerable learning, Octavius ably and eloquently defends Christianity against the blistering attack launched by the pagan Caecilius.

Of course, Felix had no tape recorder with him on the day his companions had their discussion. So what we read is not a verbatim transcript of what was actually said. Instead, it's a re-constructed version of the debate, written many years after the event. But this is to our benefit. For what results is largely a presentation of the *typical* accusations pagan Romans were making against the early Christians—and the typical Christian responses to those accusations. *Octavius* was written sometime between 150 and 210 A.D. At the time it was written, it was a crime punishable by death to even be a Christian. So Christians met in secret. This necessary secrecy fueled all sorts of rumors about Christians. Felix wrote his record of this debate in order to show the falsity of these rumors.

Unfortunately, we know little about Mark Minucius Felix, other than the fact he was a Roman lawyer and an orthodox Christian. This is sad, for unlike most other apologies, *Octavius* is a true work of literature. Felix wrote in a graceful Latin style that rivals that of Cicero. In *Octavius* he carefully builds a dramatic setting for the debate between pagan and Christian. Then he sustains the tension between the opposing views throughout the work. The defense of Christianity he presents is truly inspiring. In the end, *Octavius* is more than a challenge to the pagan Romans—it's a challenge to the twentieth century church.

As you will observe in your reading, one distinguishing mark of early Christianity was its childlike, literal adherence to the teachings of Jesus and the apostles. To the early Christian, trusting God meant more than a teary-eyed testimony about "the time I came to trust the Lord." It meant believing that even if obedience to God entailed great suffering, God was trustworthy to bring a person through it. For the early Christians, to claim to trust God while refusing to obey him was a contradiction. And they didn't feel they had to understand the reason for a commandment before they would obey it.

In our age of "easy believism," the lives of the early Christians should challenge us to move beyond mere verbal Christianity to a living, obedient relationship with God.

SUMMARY

CHARACTERS

Mark Felix: the narrator
Caecilius: Mark's companion who attacks Christianity
Octavius: Mark's friend who defends Christianity

OUTLINE

Part 1: Background and setting for the debate (ch. 1)
Part 2: Caecilius' speech against the Christians (ch. 2-3)
Part 3: Octavius' defense of Christianity (ch. 4-8)
Part 4: Conclusion (ch. 9)

1

On The Sands Of The Mediterranean

I often reflect on my memories of Octavius, my dear and loyal friend. I remember his charm and sweetness so vividly that it seems that I'm actually journeying back in time—rather than simply reminiscing about events that have long since passed. Although I can no longer actually see him with my eyes, a vivid picture of him is deeply etched into my heart. It's no wonder that I've missed this remarkable and holy man so much since he departed this life.

He radiated a deep love for me at all times, during both work and play. The things I loved, he loved. The things he disliked, I disliked. You would have thought that our two bodies shared but one mind. He was my confidant in my loves; my pillar of support in my mistakes.

And when I climbed out of the gloomy abyss of spiritual darkness into the light of wisdom and truth, he did not cast me aside. Rather, he also turned to the way of truth—and even outstripped me in his spiritual walk. For that reason, when I was recently musing over the events during our many years of intimacy and friendship, I reflected at length on our time together at the seaside resort of Ostia.* It was there that, through his skilled argumentation, he converted my com-

---

* Ostia was the ancient port of Rome, located at the mouth of the Tiber River.

panion Caecilius from pagan superstitions to the true religion.

Yes, I still remember that occasion vividly.[†] It had been a long while since Octavius and I had seen each other. But then along came some business for Octavius to attend to in Rome, which provided a good excuse for him to come and visit me. However, to do so meant being away from his wife, children, and home. This was particularly difficult for him, since one of his children was still a toddler. I know how hard it is to be away from your children during their innocent years, when they bubble out incomplete words in that precious language of their own. It's a language made more endearing by its own imperfections.

As his visit was unexpected, I was overwhelmed with joy when he arrived in Rome. We spent several days just basking in each other's presence, enjoying our mutual friendship. First, we caught up on all that had happened in our lives since we had last seen each other. Then we decided to journey to the pleasant coastal town of Ostia so I could enjoy the healthful benefits of bathing in the refreshing waters of the sea. Since it was harvest time for the vineyards, the courts were in recess. So we left immediately, and Caecilius came with us.

After arriving in Ostia, we got up early the first morning and began walking towards the beach. We deeply inhaled the invigorating sea air as we walked, so that its healthful benefits would refresh every joint and limb of our bodies. We smiled with delight as we thought about sinking our feet into the soft sand.

As we walked along, I noticed a gleaming white marble image of the god Serapis. Suddenly, Caecilius turned to the image, raised his hand to his mouth, and threw a kiss to it. (This is something the superstitious common people customarily do). Although I was a bit embarrassed by his gesture, I said nothing.[†] However, Octavius was indignant that I had said nothing.[†] So he turned to me and said rather sharply, "My brother Mark, it's not fitting for a good man like you to desert a fellow man who is constantly at your side, living with you at home and traveling with you wherever you go. You *have* deserted him, you know, by leaving him to wander in blind ignorance. I'm shocked that you tolerate his worshiping stones in broad daylight. It makes no difference that the stones have been carved into the shape of a human and crowned with garlands. You know how wrong this is. Yet by saying nothing, you partake in his error."

None of us said anything more, and we walked quietly down the road leading from the village to the sea. Soon we were shuffling through the sand along the shore. The gently breaking waves had leveled and packed the sand so smoothly that one would have thought it had been prepared for a parade. The breeze was mild, so the waves weren't crashing with great fury or spewing foam from their crests, as I have often seen them do. Still, the sea always seems to be restless, and the waves were crisply breaking with gentle curls. Octavius and I were enjoying walking along the very edge of the water, letting the tide splash over our bare feet. We marveled at how each receding wave seemed to suck the water right back into itself before the next wave surged over the wet sand.

So we ambled along the shore line, tracking the broken, crooked edge of the water. Octavius shared some interesting stories about navigation with us as we walked. After we had journeyed for a considerable distance, we decided to return along the way we had just come. So we began to walk slowly back, trying to retrace our footprints in the wet sand.

We stopped for a moment at a spot where some boats were lying at rest. They had been hoisted out of the water onto oak frameworks to preserve them from rotting. From behind the boats, we heard the laughter of children, so we followed the sound to see what was amusing them. We discovered they were playing some sort of throwing game with shells. The game went something like this: The boys would scour the shore line trying to find shells that had been rubbed smooth by the waves. When each one had found a suitable shell, he would hold it horizontally in his fingers and cock his arm back. He would then hurl his shell as low as possible, letting it skim along the tops of the waves, skipping up and down as it went. The boy whose shell went out the farthest and leaped up most frequently was declared the winner.

Octavius and I were so engrossed in watching the boys' game and sharing in their laughter that I momentarily forgot about Caecilius. Then I noticed that he was neither laughing with us nor paying any attention to the boys' game. Instead, he was standing some distance from us, his face cast down and sullen. It was obvious that he was upset about something, but I didn't know what.

"Caecilius, what's the matter?" I asked quietly. "You don't seem your usual self at all. Normally, you're the most jovial person around, even in matters that are serious."

"I'm sorry, but I found your friend's remarks rather offensive. He may have addressed his comments to *you*, but it was really *me* that he was attacking. It was *me* he was accusing of being ignorant," he said indignantly. Then lifting his voice and glancing at Octavius, he said, "This is really a matter between Octavius and me. So I'll tell you what. If he's so sure of his position, let's have a debate—like the philosophers do. Although Octavius may be able to defend his beliefs to his friends, he'll soon find they won't hold up in a heated debate."

When Octavius agreed to debate, Caecilius exclaimed, "Look! We can rest on those rocks over there and talk without being disturbed." He pointed to some large boulders that had been assembled to form a jetty into the harbor, protecting the bathing area.

When Octavius agreed that this was an ideal place to have our discussion, the three of us walked over to the rocks and climbed out over the harbor.† Finding a comfortable spot, I sat down first.† Then they sat on either side of me. The purpose of this seating arrangement wasn't to show any kind of rank or honor. For in friendship, all are equals. Rather, I sat in the middle so that I could serve as a moderator of the debate.

2

How Romans View The Christians

Caecilius began the discussion: "I realize of course, Mark, that you aren't really a neutral party. For you used to believe as I do, but some years ago you chose Christianity over our traditional beliefs. Nevertheless, in the present situation, it's your duty to serve as an impartial judge in our debate, favoring neither side. In the end, you must render a decision as to who is the winner of the debate, based solely on the arguments presented, not on your own preconceptions."

I agreed to his stipulations, and so the debate began, with Caecilius speaking first:[†]

Man Cannot Discover Absolute Truth.

"Any impartial person will agree that all things in human life are uncertain. We can't really state *anything* with absolute certainty. The most we can say is that something is *probably* true, rather than certainly true. But the mentally lazy tire from having to thoroughly investigate matters. They quickly succumb to a definite opinion about things, rather than persevering in a diligent investigation of truth.

"For that reason, all men should be indignant, or rather should be grieved, that certain people who are unlearned and illiterate dare to assert that they know the ultimate truth about the universe and the gods that be. After all, learned philosophers and multitudes of religious sects still deliberate about these matters. And for good reason! Our human intelligence is limited. We hardly have the capacity to thoroughly investigate divine matters. We aren't meant to know what's in the heavens above us or in the depths of the earth below us. We're doing well to simply know ourselves intimately, as one of the ancient sages advised. But if we're foolish enough to seek after things beyond man's knowledge, we should at least not compound our foolishness by forming dogmatic opinions about such things.

Who Says There Has To Be A Creator?

"Why do we have to bring God into the picture anyway? Couldn't all things have been combined by the forces of nature? Couldn't all the heavenly bodies be the result of the concurrence of chance accidents? Perhaps the stars were lit up by fire itself, rather than by God. Perhaps the heavenly bodies are suspended in the sky simply due to the lightness of their own composition. Maybe the earth was formed by the weight of its own materials. Perhaps the sea was made simply from the flow of moisture. So why do we have to bring religion into all of this? Why mix these things up with superstition and fear?

> *Couldn't all the heavenly bodies be the result of chance accidents?*

"Man and the animals are simply voluntary compositions of the elements. We are born, infused with life, and nourished by the elements. And we will all eventually dissipate back into the elements from which we came. All things flow back to their original source and are recycled into new things— without the help of any designer or creator.

"The seeds of fires gather together and form new suns to keep shining. The earth exhales its vapors into the air, which rise and condense to form the clouds. When these clouds begin to sink, they cause the rain to fall, the wind to blow, and the hail to pummel things below. When the clouds crash together, they cause thunder to boom, lightning to glow in the sky, and lightning bolts to shoot out. These lightning bolts hit places at random. Sometimes they hit a mountain, other times, a tree. There's no direction or purpose to them. Sometimes they blast a sacred building, other times a profane place. Sometimes they strike wrongdoers; other times they strike holy men.

"The same principle is true of storms. They attack all things without discrimination. In shipwrecks, the destinies of good and bad men are jumbled together. They suffer the same end. When fire strikes a city or a building, the innocent and guilty are united in the same death. When a plague strikes, all people perish without distinction. In battle, it is usually the more noble men who are killed.

"If the world were governed by divine care or by the authority of any kind of God, evil rulers like Dionysius would never have deserved to reign. Righteous men like Camillus would never have been banished. Seekers of truth like Socrates would never have been forced to drink poison.

"Right now the fruit trees are laden with fruit ready to be picked. The golden grain stands ready for harvest. The grapes are ripe and about to fall from the vines. Yet before they're harvested, rain may ruin them. They may be beaten down by hail. So either there are Beings governing the universe whom we know little about, or more likely, the world is governed by mere chance, by blind fortune that knows no laws.

Christians Should Learn From The Philosophers.

"However, if you have a desire to philosophize, let one of your teachers try to imitate Socrates, the prince of wisdom. Everyone knows that when Socrates was once asked about heavenly things, he answered, 'What's above us is nothing to us.' He well deserved the acclamation of the oracle who said that Socrates was the greatest of men—not because he had discovered all things, but because he had learned that he knew nothing. The confession of ignorance is the height of wisdom.

"When a certain ruler asked Simonides what he thought the gods were like, he asked permission to think about it for a day. The next day, he said he needed an additional day to consider the matter. At the end of the second day, he requested still another. Finally, the ruler grew impatient and demanded to know the reason for the delay. Simonides replied, 'The more I think about the matter, the less I realize I really know about the gods.'

"I agree with him. Things that are uncertain ought to be left as they are. Furthermore, when so many great men are deliberating about the matter, we shouldn't rashly introduce new opinions from the opposite direction. In doing so, we are likely, at best, only to introduce a childish superstition. At worst, we may end up overthrowing all religion.

"Therefore, since either fortune is certain or nature is uncertain, how much wiser and more reverent it is, as high priests of truth, to accept the teachings of your ancestors that were handed down to you. How much better to *fear* the gods your parents taught you to worship than to try to *know* these gods intimately. Rather than trying to discover some new view of the gods, it's far better to accept the teachings of our ancient forefathers. They lived at a time when the world was new. They deserved to have gods as their kings. For that reason, we can observe that throughout all the empires, provinces, and cities of the world, each people group has its own national rites of worship. Each group worships its local gods. The Chaldeans worship Bel. The Syrians, Astarte. The Phrygians, the Great Mother. The Taurians, Diana. And the Gauls, Mercury.

> *It's far better to accept the teachings of our ancient forefathers.*

Rome Has Conquered Because It Worships All Gods.

"However, we Romans worship *all* gods. That's the reason we have authority and power over the circuit of the entire world. That's why we've expanded our empire beyond the paths of the sun—beyond the boundaries of the ocean itself. We arm ourselves with religious fervor. We fortify Rome with sacred rites, chaste virgins, and priests. We actively seek out gods of strangers and make them our own. When we conquer a city, we immediately worship the gods of that conquered city. We Romans moved right through the lines of the Gauls, unarmed with weapons, but armed with the worship of the Gauls' very own gods. We even build altars to unknown gods. So we Romans deserve our dominion over all nations, because we acknowledge the sacred religions of all nations.

"When you consult the books of our ancestors, you discover that they have instituted the rites of all sorts of religions. These rites ensure the blessings of the gods. They keep the gods from becoming angry. And if the gods are already angry, the sacred rites appease their wrath. The city of Rome is protected by the many temples of the gods that are in it. And the gods themselves dwell in these temples. As a result, the oracles of the temples—filled with a particular god—are able to foretell the future. They can thwart dangers, provide cures for diseases, give hope to the afflicted, and offer solace after calamities. Although we may impiously deny and renounce the gods during the daytime, we see, hear, and acknowledge the gods in our rest."

3

Dark Rumors About The Christians

Caecilius continued, "Since all nations recognize the existence of the immortal gods (even though their nature and origin are uncertain), how can anyone be so rash as to undermine the ancient religions! What type of sacrilegious wisdom would attack these religions that are so helpful and wholesome?

"The men of Athens once expelled a certain philosopher and publicly burned his writings. Why? Merely because he disputed about the gods. So how much more should we lament the fact that an illegal, depraved, and desperate group of men who are called 'Christians' should attack the gods! To make matters worse, they have added to their numbers unskilled men from the dregs of society and women, who are gullible and yielding because of their sex.

> *You despise present torments, but you fear those that are future.*

This profane conspiracy is united by its nightly meetings, solemn fasts, and inhuman meats [i.e. cannibalism]. You Christians are a skulking people who shun the light. You say nothing in public, but you babble endlessly in private corners.

"You despise the temples as houses of the dead. You reject the gods and laugh at sacred things. You pity the priests. Half-naked yourselves, you despise honors and purple robes. What incredible folly! What audacity! You despise present torments, but you fear those that are uncertain and future. While you don't fear to die for the present, you fear to die after death.

You Eat Babies And Revel In Orgies.

"And now as the world grows more wicked, your abominable shrines are sprouting up throughout the whole world. This entire impious confederacy should be rooted out and destroyed! You know one another by secret marks and insignia. You love one another almost before you know one another. Yours is a religion of lust. You promiscuously call one another brothers and sisters. You apparently do this so that your debaucheries will take on the flavor of incest. Your vain and senseless superstition revels in wickedness. I would apologize for passing on the reports I hear about you if I weren't so certain that they are true.*

"For example, I hear that you worship the head of a donkey, the lowest of all creatures. But I suppose that's fitting for such a religion as yours. Some say you worship the genitals of your priests. I don't know whether these things are true or not. But it's only natural that your secret, nocturnal rites would arouse suspicion. Especially since you adore a wicked man who was punished by suffering excruciating pain on the deadly wood of a cross. Yet I suppose that crosses are fitting altars for depraved and wicked men. In short, you worship what you deserve.

"The stories of your initiation rites are as detestable as they are well known. Your priests place an infant covered with flour in front of the new convert. Then they tell the convert

---

* This chapter reveals what Romans commonly belived about Christians. Many of their conceptions were false. The rumors about cannibalism evidently came from their hearing that Christians partook of the "body and blood" of Christ at their meetings. Hearing about "love feasts," the exchange of the "holy kiss," and the designation of each other as "brother" and "sister," Romans commonly thought that Christians engaged in incestuous orgies.

to strike the harmless-looking lump of flour with deadly blows. Thereby the convert innocently slays the infant and is initiated into your horrors. The Christians present then lick up the infant's blood and divide its limbs among themselves to eat. They are united by this unholy meal, since they are bound to mutual silence because of their wickedness. Your sacred rites are more vile than any imagined sacrilege.

"Your banquets are also well known and are spoken about everywhere. On a solemn day, all of you assemble together at the feast, along with your children, sisters, and mothers. People of every sex and age are present. After much feasting, when the group is boisterous and when incestuous lust has grown hot with drunkenness, you throw a piece of meat just outside the reach of a dog that has been tied to the room's lamp. In trying to reach the meat, the dog overturns the lamp and plunges the room into darkness. The incestuous lusts of those present are now unfettered, and nature takes its course in the dark.

"Time doesn't permit me to discuss all the things known about your rites. But the fact that your religion is so secret and obscure verifies that most—if not all—of the things I've related are true. If not, why do you go to such lengths to conceal whatever it is you worship? Honorable things are done out in the open. Only crimes are kept secret. Why do you have no altars, temples, or images? Why do you never speak openly or congregate freely? It must be that your worship is either something that deserves punishment or something that's shameful.

You Worship A Busybody God.

"Who is this one God you claim to worship? He seems to be solitary and desolate. No free people, no kingdoms—not even Roman religious traditions know anything about him. The lonely and miserable nation of the Jews worshiped one God—a God peculiar to themselves. But at least they worshiped him openly with temples, altars, sacrifices, and ceremonies. But he had so little power that he is enslaved, along with his peculiar nation, to the Roman gods.

"How absurd, therefore, that you Christians claim that this God of yours, whom you can neither show to others or see yourselves, is somehow earnestly concerned about everyone's character and deeds. You even say he looks into everyone's words and secret thoughts. He supposedly runs about everywhere and is present everywhere. You make him out to be troublesome, restless, and shamelessly inquisitive. Obviously, if he is present at everything that's done, and wanders in and out of every place, he can't give attention to the particulars. He's too busy with the whole. But if he is busy with particulars, he obviously can't take care of the whole.

You Teach Fables About The End Of The World And Death.

"How foolish that you preach that the whole world—in fact, the whole universe with all its stars—is going to burn up. As if the eternal and divine laws of nature could be disturbed. Or the union of all elements could be broken up. Or the fabric that holds together the entire heavenly structure could be overthrown.

"And you are not content with merely this wild opinion. So you add old wive's tales to it, saying you will rise again after death—after you have returned to dust and ashes. You believe these lies with such confidence that a person would suppose you had already been raised from the dead. How absurd to proclaim that the heavens and stars, which are unchanging from generation to generation, will eventually be destroyed, particularly when you promise eternity to us humans, who so quickly perish.

"Apparently that's why you Christians denounce our funeral pyres and reject cremation. But what difference should they make? Don't you realize that a body buried in the ground returns to the earth within a few years? So it doesn't matter whether a body is torn to pieces by wild beasts or drowned in the sea, whether it's buried in the ground or consumed by fire. No matter how you dispose of a corpse, if the corpse feels it, it's a form of punishment. But if the corpse doesn't feel it, it's a blessing to destroy it quickly.

"Deceived by your errors, you promise yourselves a blessed and perpetual life after death, since you view yourselves as righteous. On the other hand, viewing others as unrighteous, you promise them eternal punishment. However, I think I've already established that you are clearly *not* righteous. But if, for the sake of argument, I conceded that you are righteous, your views are still similar to many non-Christian teachers who teach that guilt and innocence are determined by fate. What most people attribute to fate, you attribute to God. You teach that men don't act of their own accord, but as they are elected to act. So you set up a wicked Judge, who punishes us, not for our *deeds*, but for our *destiny*.

"Still, I would like to know whether or not you're going to rise again with physical bodies. If so, will they be the same bodies you died in? Or will they be renewed bodies? You can hardly say you'll rise with the same body, for that body has already decayed. But if you say it's with another body, then it's a *new man* who is born. The original man is not being restored. And if you say that you'll arise without any body, then as far as I can see, there will be neither mind, soul, nor life.

"But why even speculate about such things?† Innumerable ages have passed since the beginning of man. Yet not one single individual has ever returned from the dead. Not even for a few *hours*. Certainly, no one has returned to live again as an example for belief. So your teachings are simply the figment of an unhealthy mind. A false hope for comfort. It's bad enough that the deceiving poets trifled with such imaginary things for the sake of poetic beauty. But it's disgraceful that you have re-created such teachings, believing so gullibly in your God.

> *The majority of you are in want, are cold, and are hungry.*

"Why don't you at least learn from your present situation how vain your expectations are? Your present lot should tell you what you can expect after death. Many of you—in fact, by your own admission, the majority of you—are in want, are cold, are hungry, and are laboring in hard work. Yet your God allows it. So he's either unwilling or unable to assist his people. In other words, he's either weak or unjust. You dream about immortality after death. Can't you see the truth about your situation when you are shaken by danger? When you are burning with fever? When you are torn with pain? Doesn't this make you realize the truth of your own frailty?

You Miss All The Fun In Life.

"But why talk about things that are common to *all* humans? You don't even fare as well as the rest of mankind.† Instead, you face threats, punishments, tortures, and crosses. Not crosses for you to *venerate*, but crosses for you to be *tortured* on. And fires too. Where is the God who is supposed to help you when you come back from the dead? He can't even help you in this life! Don't the Romans, without any help from your God, rule over the whole world? Don't we have dominion over you yourselves?

"In the meantime, living in suspense and anxiety, you abstain from respectable pleasures. You don't visit exhibitions. You have no interest in public displays. You reject the public banquets and abhor the sacred games. You refuse the meats and drinks offered on our altars. So, actually, you stand in fear of the very gods you deny. You refuse to crown your heads with wreaths of flowers and to anoint your bodies with perfume. Instead, you reserve perfume for your funeral rites. But you refuse flower wreaths even for your coffins. Look at you! Pale, trembling wretches. You deserve to be pitied by our gods!

"Thus, wretched as you are, you will neither rise from the dead, nor enjoy life in the meantime. So, if you have any wisdom or sense, stop prying into the heavens and the destinies and secrets of the world. It's enough for untaught, uncultivated, boorish, and rustic people to watch where they're stepping. People who are unable to understand civil matters are certainly unable to discuss divine ones!"

4

We Believe All People Are Equal

Having reached the end of his discourse, Caecilius gloated. Perhaps the vehemence of his speech had worked off some of his initial anger. Sitting down and mopping his brow,† he added, smiling proudly, "And what does Octavius venture to reply to this! You're like Plautus—chief of the millers, but lowest of the philosophers."

"Wait a minute!" I interjected. "Before you start boasting about your grand discourse, you'd better wait until both sides are presented. Especially since you claim you're seeking truth, rather than the applause of men. I'll be the first to admit that your arguments have intrigued me. But at the same time, I'm not comfortable with this whole process of debating. Does truth change merely because of the eloquence of the speaker or the power of his delivery?

> *Something can sound very logical and still be false.*

"I fear that most listeners are swayed by the beauty or power of words rather than by their truth. Something can sound very logical and still be false. Or something may sound unbelievable and be true. Unfortunately, people tend to accept something as true simply because it's boldly asserted. So they are deceived both by the cleverness of the speaker and by their own foolhardiness.

"Others would rather leave all questions unanswered, instead of pondering over matters that aren't clear. But surely we don't want to become like them and reject all teaching. Nor do we want to end up hating and distrusting everyone. For those who are gullible are often deceived by those they trusted. Once they realize this, they begin to suspect that everyone is a deceiver. They then reject people they would have otherwise viewed with respect.

"It's important that we carefully weigh everything that's said so that we approve and adopt only the things that are true. For there are two sides to every argument, and truth is sometimes hard to discern. Furthermore, the abundance of words can sometimes appear to be solid proof, but it really isn't."

"I think you've forgotten that you're supposed to be an impartial judge," Caecilius interrupted. "It's not fair for you to try to weaken the force of my argument by interjecting other matters. Octavius has in front of him everything I said. It's up to *him* to refute my words."

"But I only mentioned these things for the common benefit of all of us," I explained in my own defense. "We want to reach our decision by a scrupulous examination of the truth itself, not by the pompous style or eloquence of the speaker. But rather than belaboring this point, let's hear what Octavius has to say in reply."

Octavius Defends Christianity.

Rising slowly, Octavius smiled and began: "I will indeed answer Caecilius to the best of my ability. And please excuse me if my words become too sharp at any point.

"First, let me say that it seems to me, Caecilius, that your position has swayed back and forth erratically in a rather slippery manner. I'm not sure whether your information was simply confused, or if you didn't realize that you kept shifting your position. One moment you seemed to believe in the gods; the next moment, you weren't sure. I don't know which position to address, since your position kept changing.

"I don't think you did this intentionally for the purpose of confusing me. Rather, I think you're more like the traveler who came to a multi-laned fork in the road. He didn't know which road to take, and he was hardly able to try them all. So he just sat there confused. Caecilius, I see you as a person cast about by the tide, tossed hither and thither by opinions that are contrary to one another. I want to help you find the right way, so I will answer everything you've said, no matter how diverse. In the end, I will confirm the truth alone, so that you no longer need to doubt and waiver.

"My brother, you said that you were grieved and vexed that illiterate, poor, and unskilled people should dispute about heavenly things. You should know that all people are born alike, with a capacity and ability to reason and feel—regardless of their age, sex, or position in life. People don't obtain wisdom by fortune, it's implanted by nature. Furthermore, even the eminent philosophers themselves were originally viewed as ignorant, half-naked peasants, before their mental skill earned them recognition.

> *All people are born alike, with a capacity to reason and feel— regardless of their age, sex, or position in life.*

"Actually, rich people, who are married to their wealth, spend more time looking at their gold than looking to heaven. [Luke 18:25] On the other hand, our sort of people, although poor, have not only discovered wisdom, but have taught it to others. So intelligence is not something you can buy with wealth, nor obtain by study. Rather it's conceived when the mind is formed. Therefore, you have no cause to be angry because someone inquires about, and expresses his thoughts about, divine things. After all, the important thing is the truth of the argument, not the authority of the speaker. In fact, the more unpretentious the discourse, the more evident the reasoning. Since it isn't colored by the pomp of eloquence and grace, it is sustained by its own truth."

5

Why We Believe In One God

Octavius continued, "But I agree with you, Caecilius, that man should know himself. He should look around and see what he is. Why he is. And where he came from. Was he collected together from the elements? Was he harmoniously formed of atoms?* Or was he created and given life by God? We can't answer these questions about man unless we first inquire about the universe. All these things are interconnected. You can't understand the nature of humanity unless you first examine the nature of divinity.

"How can a person perform his social duty if he doesn't understand the common bonds of all mankind? Man is different from the wild beasts. Their faces are always looking down at the earth, gazing at their food. But man stands erect. His face is turned toward heaven. His thoughts and his conversation are of heaven. For this reason, we recognize, feel, and imitate God. No person has the right or reason to be ignorant of the celestial glory that's imprinted on our eyes and senses. [Rom. 1:20] It's wrong to seek on earth what can only be found on high.

---

* The theory that matter is made up of atoms was developed hundreds of years before Christ by the Greek philosophers Leucippus, Democritus, and Epicurus.

"So it seems to me that those people who say that the whole universe was heaped together by certain atoms casually adhering to each other—denying that it was formed by the divine Logos*—have neither mind nor sense. Apparently, they don't even have the ability to *see*. For what can be more obvious when you lift your eyes up to the sky, and look around at the things here on earth, than that there is some Deity of supreme intelligence who governs and nourishes the universe, infusing it with life?

"Take the heavens, for example. Notice how far they reach and how rapidly the heavenly bodies move around. See how the sky is adorned by the stars at night and how the sun illuminates it during the day. Surely the marvelous and divine balance of the Supreme Governor is at work here. [Ps. 136:1-9] Look also at the year, how it is made by the circuit of the sun. And look at the month, how the moon formulates it with its phases

> *You can't under-stand the nature of humanity unless you examine the nature of divinity.*

of increase and decrease. Or how about the recurring pattern of day and night, which provides man with a time for work and a time for rest?

"I will have to leave it to the astronomers to discuss the stars in more detail: how they guide navigators and how they indicate the times to plow and harvest. Surely, a Supreme Artist and a Perfect Intelligence was needed to create and arrange these things. In fact, it takes a lot of intelligence just to *understand* them.

"What about the regular change of the seasons? The spring with its flowers. The summer with its harvests. The pleasing maturity of autumn. And winter, the time to gather olives. These changes of season are essential. Yet unless they were established by the highest intelligence, they would be easily

---

* i.e., Jesus. In Greek, Logos means both Word and Reason.

disturbed. How dependent we are on God's provisions. Otherwise, there might be nothing but winter to blast us with its frost. Or summer, to scorch us with its heat. Instead, we have the moderate temperatures of autumn and spring to separate winter and summer. This way, the gradual transitions of the year glide by, year after year.

"Look also at the sea. It's bound by the law of its shore. And notice the ocean, with its regular ebb and flow of tides. [Job 38:4-11] Look also at the trees, how they are sustained from the depths of the earth. And the fountains, how they gush in perpetual streams. Gaze at the rivers. See how they flow on their same course, year after year. And I haven't even mentioned the ordered peaks of the mountains, the slopes of the hills, and the expanses of the plains.

"I could point to the different types of protection provided for the animals. Some are armed with horns; others with teeth. Some have claws; others are barbed with stingers. Some escape danger by the swiftness of their feet, others by soaring into the sky with their wings.

"Finally, the very beauty of our own bodies confesses that God is their designer. Our upright stature and countenance. [Ps. 139:14] The placement of our eyes at the top of our bodies, like a lookout. And the arrangement of the rest of our senses like a citadel. Every member of the body has been designed both for the sake of necessity and for beauty. What's even more wonderful is that even though we all have essentially the same bodies, we don't all look alike.

"What's the purpose of our being born? Where does the drive to procreate come from? Why do the breasts become full of milk just as the baby is ready to be born? Surely God arranged it this way so that the infant would have food for nourishment.

"But God not only cares for the universe as a *whole*, he's equally concerned about its *parts*. For example, Britain doesn't receive much sunshine, but it's refreshed by the warmth of the sea that flows around it. Egypt is dry, but its dryness is tempered by the presence of the Nile River. Arid

Mesopotamia is irrigated by the Euphrates River. The River Indus is said to both sow and water the East.

"Now, if upon entering a house you found everything well arranged and adorned, you would surely believe that a master governed the house. You would also recognize that the master was greater than all of the things in the house. Therefore, when you look upon the house of the universe—the heavens and the earth, its laws, and its order—believe that there is a Lord and Parent of the universe far more glorious than the stars themselves and the other parts of the universe.

There Can Only Be One God.

"Since it's obvious that a Creator exists, the next question is whether the celestial kingdom is governed by one or by many. To answer this question, we only have to look at the empires here on earth, which are no doubt patterned after the heavenly example. When has there ever been an alliance of royal authority that started in good faith and continued without bloodshed? Look at Pompey and his father-in-law, Caesar. Their wars were scattered over the whole earth; even the vast Roman empire could not accommodate two rulers. Look also at nature. The bees have one ruler and so do the flocks and herds.

He is purer than the sense of touch; he is greater than all perceptions.

"So how can you believe that there is a division of divine power in heaven or that the authority of the true and divine empire is splintered? It's obvious that God, the Parent of all, has neither beginning nor end. [1 Tim. 1:17] He who gives birth to all possesses immortality for himself. He orders everything in the universe by his word. [Ps. 33:6] He arranges it by his wisdom. He perfects it by his power. He cannot be seen, for he is brighter than light. He cannot be touched, for he is purer than the sense of touch. He cannot even be estimated, for he is greater than all perceptions. He is infinite, immense. Only he understands his own greatness, for our minds are too limited to understand him. We make a worthy estimate when we say he is beyond estimation. [Rom. 11:33,34] The man who thinks he knows the magnitude of God actually diminishes his magnitude.

"Neither should you ask what God's name is. *God* is his name. Names are only needed when there is a multitude of beings and you must distinguish them. But for God, who is alone, the name God is sufficient. If I were to call him Father, you would think him to be earthly. If I called him King, you would think of him as flesh and blood. If I called him Lord, you would surely think of him as mortal. But take away the addition of names, and you will behold his glory.

"But this should not seem strange to you. I often hear the common people lift their hands to heaven and simply say, 'Oh God!' or 'God is great,' or 'God is true,' or 'if God permits.' I often wonder whether I'm hearing the prayer of a confessing Christian or the natural speech of the common people. Furthermore, many say that Jupiter is supreme over all. So they're essentially in agreement with us, although they're mistaken about the name."

6

Running Naked In Winter—And Other Roman Religious Customs

Octavius continued, "As for your gods, even the dumb animals know the truth about them. Mice and birds know they have no feeling. They perch on them, walk over them, and even gnaw on them. In fact, unless you drive them away, they will build their nests in the mouths of your gods. Spiders will weave their webs over the face of a god and suspend threads from its head. First you make your own gods, then you have to clean and protect them. For some reason, you don't realize that you must *know* God before you can *worship* him. [John 17:3] You choose to follow the traditions of your ancestors, simply compounding their errors, rather than trusting in your own ability to reason. You fear gods without even knowing them.

> You must know God before you can worship him.

"And if you stand aside and take an honest look at the rites of these gods, you will soon realize how pitiful and laughable they are. Naked people run about in the raw of winter. Others walk around with elaborate bonnets, carrying old shields and beating on drums. Others lead their gods on a begging expedition through the streets. People are permitted to approach some temples only once a year; others are completely closed to visitors. There is one place where a man may not go, and there are some that are closed to women. It's considered a *crime* for a slave to be present at some ceremonies. Some sacred places are crowned by a woman having one husband; some, by a woman with many. The woman who has committed the most adulteries is sought after with great religious zeal.

"What about the men who supplicate their gods by cutting themselves and offering their own blood? [1 Kings 18:28] Wouldn't it be better for such men to be unreligious than to practice such a religion? And those who seek to supplicate God by cutting off their private parts are greatly wronging God. If God had wanted eunuchs, he would have brought them into existence as such. He wouldn't make them eunuchs afterwards.

"Isn't it obvious that people who practice all these things are foolish and of unsound mind? Their only defense seems to be that everyone else is doing it.

Rome Has Prospered At The Expense Of Others.

"Nevertheless, you have claimed that such superstition is the very thing that established and increased the Roman empire. You say that the Romans conquered, not so much by their valor, but by their religion and reverence. You would agree, no doubt, that this 'illustrious and noble justice of the Romans' was present when the nation was founded. But didn't the Romans originally come together and fortify themselves by *crime*? Didn't they grow by the terror of their own fierceness? The first Romans were a flock of assassins, traitors, wanderers, criminals, and incest-mongers. Romulus, their commander and governor, killed his own brother. So he was even more evil than his followers. And you describe this as a religious state?

"But the Romans grew even worse with time.† Next, they kidnapped and raped foreign virgins—some of whom were already engaged to husbands. They even kidnapped married women to be their wives—something unparalleled in wantonness. Later, they went to war against their own fathers-in-law, shedding the blood of their own kinsmen. What could be more irreligious and presumptuous? The Romans found safety in their own wanton criminality.

> *Rome grew by the loss of others.*

They drove their own neighbors from the land. They overthrew nearby cities, including their temples and altars, and sent the people into captivity. In short, Rome grew by the *loss* of others. Romulus, the founder of Rome, instituted this principle, and it has continued through the present day.

"So the possessions of you Romans are really the spoils of your audacity. Your temples were built from the plunder of your violence. You have murdered priests. You insult and scorn the gods of others by vanquishing their peoples. You only venerate these gods once you have captured them. To worship what you have taken by force is to consecrate sacrilege, not piety. So the Romans didn't become great because they were *religious*, but because they were *sacrilegious* with impunity.

"Anyway, how could such conquered gods be of help to the Romans? They obviously weren't able to help their own worshipers against the Roman armies.

Your Fortunetellers Are Inspired By Demons.

"As for your diviners and oracles, I will acknowledge that sometimes they have been close to the truth in their predictions. Of course, this might simply be a matter of chance rather than foreknowledge. After all, after making so many wrong predictions, the odds are that the diviners and oracles would sometimes guess correctly. However, I think there may be more to it than that. So let's look into the matter more deeply, to find the actual source of error and evil.

"If we dig deep enough, we find that there are certain deceptive, wandering spirits who have been degraded from their heavenly station by earthly stains and lusts. [2 Pet. 2:4] Now that they have corrupted themselves, they seek to corrupt others. [1 Tim. 4:1] And being alienated from God themselves, they try to alienate others from God by introducing degraded superstitions. The poets know that those spirits are demons. The philosophers talk about them, too. Socrates knew about them, for he undertook various affairs based upon the decisions of a demon who was at his side.

"The Magi also know that there are demons. What's more, they perform their miracles by means of demons. One of these Magi named Sosthenes once described the true God with all His majesty. He also talked about the angels who are the ministers and messengers of God. He even taught that the demons are earthly, wandering spirits who are hostile to mankind.

"You have mentioned Plato, who said that discovering God is difficult. He spoke without hesitation about both angels and demons. In his work entitled *Symposium*, he tried to explain the nature of demons. He said they are of a substance somewhere between mortal and immortal, between body and spirit, between heavenly and earthly.

"These demons lurk in your temples among the idols. The Magi, the philosophers, and Plato all showed this. The demons inspire the prophets who dwell among their shrines. Sometimes they animate the entrails of animals that diviners search through for prophetic clues. Other times, they control the flight of birds or the casting of lots. They're the reason many falsehoods are spoken by the oracles. For they are both deceivers and deceived. They weigh men down, pulling them away from heaven. They lure people from God to material things.

Jupiter Is Really A Demon.

"They also creep secretly into human bodies as though they were spirits. Then they feign diseases, disturb the mind, and wrench about the limbs of the possessed person. [Luke

9:37-42] However, when sacrifices are made to them, they often set the possessed person free. So it appears that these demon gods have *cured* the illness, when actually they *caused* it. This is how they attract worshipers.

"Many people, including Romans, have heard the demons confess to such things once they have been driven out of someone by our words and prayers. Saturn, Serapis, Jupiter, and whatever other demons you worship, overcome by the torment of our words and the pain of our prayers, openly speak out about who they are. They obviously would not lie to their own discredit, especially when non-Christians are standing by. Since they themselves confess they're demons, believe them when they confess the truth about themselves. For when they are denounced by the one true God, the wretched beings shudder in their bodies. They then either leap out at once or vanish by degrees, depending on the assisting faith of the possessed one or the inspiring grace of the healer.

"The demons, with your help, may harass Christians from a *distance*, but they flee from us when near at hand. [Jas. 4:7] So they attack us by possessing the minds of the ignorant and sowing seeds of hatred against us. Blinding the minds and hearts of men, the demons cause them to hate us before they even know us. For they realize that once people know the truth about us, they will want to imitate us. At the very least, they won't be able to condemn us."

7

What Christians Are Really Like

Octavius continued, "How wrong it is, therefore, for you to form a judgment about things you haven't examined and know little about. Yet at one time we thought the same things you do, when we were blind and in darkness. Like others, I once thought that Christians worshiped monsters, ate infants, and mingled in incestuous banquets. I didn't realize that those were fables invented by gossips and that they had never been examined or proved. I didn't realize that in the decades since the beginning of Christianity, no Christian had ever come forward to betray the evil things that Christians were supposedly doing, seeking pardon for his crimes and a reward for having publicly revealed such things. I never took notice of the fact that when a Christian was accused, he never blushed at having done vile things. He never feared punishment. Instead, he only regretted that he had not become a Christian sooner.

"Even when we took pity on the Christians, we were cruel in our pity. We tortured them when they confessed Christ, so that by denying him they might save their lives. What perverted justice! Instead of trying to elicit *truth*, we were trying to force them to *lie*. And if anyone denied that he was a Christian, having been overcome by the suffering due to his weakness, we showed him favor. We treated such persons as having atoned for all their alleged wrongs simply by denying the name of Christ. So you can see that I and many others felt and acted the same way that you do.

We Worship Neither A Criminal Nor His Cross.

"When you accuse us of worshiping a criminal and his cross, you are very far from the truth. How could any criminal—or any other human, for that matter—be believed to be deity? Any person who places his whole trust on mortal man is pitiable indeed, for all of his hope is extinguished when the man dies. [Ps. 146:3,4]

"For example, the Egyptians select a man to worship and pray to. They consult with him about all things and even offer sacrifices to him. And although others view him as a god, that person is still simply a man whether he likes it or not. He can fool others, but he can't fool himself. Similarly, princes and kings are often esteemed as gods, not merely as great men (which would be just). Their subjects invoke their deity, they pray to their images, and implore the "genius" of the emperor, that is, his demon. In fact, it's safer to swear falsely by the genius of Jupiter than by the genius of the emperor.

"As for crosses, we neither worship them nor wish for them. Rather, it's you, who worship gods of wood, who perhaps venerate wooden crosses as parts of your gods. Your military standards and banners are nothing more than crosses that are decorated and covered with gold. Your trophies of victory not only resemble a cross, but even a cross with a man affixed to it. The figure of the cross can also be seen in a ship when it's carried along with swelling sails, or when it glides forward with expanded oars. Also, when the military yoke is lifted up, it's in the shape of a cross. Likewise, when a man adores God with a pure mind, with hands outstretched, he forms the sign of the cross. So the sign of the cross seems to either appear naturally or else your own religion is formulated around it.

We Believe Abortion Is Murder.

"And now I would like to meet the man who says or believes that we initiate our members by slaughtering an infant. How could anyone spill the blood of one so tender? No one could believe such a thing unless he would dare do it himself. And I notice that sometimes you Romans abandon your new-born babies to wild beasts and birds. Others strangle their infants to death. There are some women who, by drinking medical potions, extinguish the source of the future man in their very bowels and thus commit murder before they give birth.

> *Some women, by drinking medical potions, extinguish the future man in their bowels and thus commit murder.*

"All of these practices actually come from the teachings about your gods. In fact, your gods act worse than you do.[†] For example, Saturn did not merely expose his children; he *ate* them. No wonder that parents in some parts of Africa sacrificed their babies to him, diligently suppressing their crying with caresses and kisses so that a weeping victim wouldn't be sacrificed. Among some peoples in Pontus and Egypt, it was a sacred rite to sacrifice their guests to their gods. The people of Gaul made human sacrifices—or should I say *inhuman* sacrifices—to Mercury. The Roman worshipers would bury alive a Greek man and woman, along with a Gallic man and woman. To this very day, they worship Jupiter Latiaris by murdering humans.

"I believe that it was Jupiter himself who taught people to heal epilepsy with human blood—that is, with a worse disease. And people who eat the wild animals from the arena, smeared with human blood and engorged with the limbs and entrails of humans, are just like Jupiter. However, for us it is unlawful to either see or hear of killing humans. So much do we shrink from human blood that we do not even use the blood of edible animals in our food.*

We Live Modest And Chaste Lives.

"As for the charge of incestuous banquets, this fable was devised by demons in order to stain the glory of our modesty. They hoped that by falsely branding us with a moral outrage, people would turn away from us before ever inquiring into the truth. But such incestuous deeds originated from your own nations, not from Christians. For example, a promiscuous association between mother and sons is allowed among the Persians. Among the Egyptians and Athenians, marriages between brothers and sisters are legitimate. The dramas that you read and enjoy seeing performed often center on incest.

"You even worship incestuous gods, who have sexual relations with their mothers, daughters, and sisters. No wonder incest abounds among you! Furthermore, many men commit incest without even knowing it. For they scatter their lusts promiscuously, fathering their children everywhere. And they even abandon their legitimate children along the roadside, letting them be taken and reared by others. So in the end, they may unknowingly be having promiscuous relations with their grown children.

> **Many of us remain virgins our entire lives.**

"As for us, our modesty is not a matter of outward show. Rather, in our hearts we gladly abide by the bonds of a single marriage. In the desire to procreate, we know either one wife or none at all. In our banquets, we share our food with one another. Not only are our banquets modest, they are also

---

*At the council in Jerusalem, the apostles wrote the church, "It seemed good to the Holy Spirit and to us to lay upon you no greater burden than these essentials: that you abstain from things sacrificed to idols and from blood and from things strangled and from fornication." (Acts 15:28,29 NAS) Although most churches today treat the apostles' injunction as a temporary command, the early Christians understood it to be a binding command for all times. *See also* Tertullian *Apology* 9; Origen *Against Celsus* 8.30.

sober. For we do not prolong our feasts with wine or indulge in entertainments. Rather, we temper our joy with serious-ness, with chaste conversation, and with bodies even more chaste. [Eph. 5:3,4] In fact, many of us remain virgins our entire lives. [Matt. 19:10-12; 1 Cor. 7:26-34] We *enjoy* our virginity rather than boasting about it. We are so far from indulging in incestuous lusts that some of us blush about even modest intermingling of the sexes.

We Reject The Honors Of This World.

"And just because we refuse your honors and purple robes doesn't mean that you should view us as the lowest of people. We are easy to please. We assemble together with the same quietness with which we live our personal lives. [Rom. 12:18] You say that we are talkative only in corners, but the truth is that you are afraid to hear us in public. The fact that our numbers increase day by day is no cause to criticize us; it is instead a praiseworthy testimony. We keep our members because we live an unblemished lifestyle, and we increase our numbers by the addition of new converts.

"Furthermore, we do not recognize our members by some small bodily mark, as you have claimed. Rather, we know one another by the signs of innocence and modesty. To your regret, we love one another with a mutual love, because we do not know how to hate. [John 13:35] To your envy, we call one another brothers, for we are all born of one God—one Parent. We are companions in faith and fellow-heirs in hope. In contrast, you don't recognize one another, and you're cruel in your mutual hatreds. You cer-tainly don't view one another as brothers, unless it's for the purpose of fratricide."

> *We love one another with a mutual love, because we do not know how to hate.*

8

God, Eternal Punishment, And Fate

Octavius explained further, "You mistakenly think we conceal what we worship simply because we have no temples or altars. Yet how can anyone make an image of God? Man himself is the image of God. How can anyone build a temple to him, when the whole world can't contain him? [1 Kings 8:27] Even I, a mere human, travel far and wide. So how can anyone shut up the majesty of so great a person within one small building? Isn't it better for him to be dedicated in our minds and consecrated in our innermost hearts—rather than in a building?

"And what sense does it make for us to offer sacrifices to the Lord? He has given us such things for our use. Should we then throw his own gifts back to him? Therefore, he who cultivates innocence is thereby supplicating God. He who sows justice makes an offering to God. He who refrains from dishonesty offers an appeasement to God. And he who rescues a fellow human from danger has offered up a most acceptable sacrificial victim to God. These are the sacrifices we Christians make. These are our sacred rites of

> *He who sows justice makes an offering to God.*

worship to God. So among us, the person who is the most just is deemed the one who is the most religious.

God Is Invisible And Present Everywhere.

"We can neither see nor display the God we worship. And it's for this very reason that we believe him to be God. We are conscious of his presence, but we can't see him. We behold his ever-present power when he thunders and sends out lightning bolts—or when he makes everything bright again. It shouldn't bother you that you can't see God. You can't see the breezes and storm winds. But they move and shake all things. Even though the sun furnishes light to see all things, you can't look directly at the sun. If you do, you'll soon lose sight altogether. So how do you think you could gaze directly at the Architect of the sun himself—the final source of all light? [Ex. 33:20] You even turn away from his lightning bolts and hide from his thunderclaps. Do you wish to see God with your physical eyes, when you can't even see your own soul, which gives you life and enables you to speak?

"Some say that God doesn't know what men are doing. Since he is far off in heaven, they say he can't see or know all individuals here on earth. How blind! What is "far off" to God? He knows all things heavenly and earthly. [Ps. 139:1,7]

> *To God this whole world is one family.*

He knows things beyond our universe. All things are full of God. He is not only very near to us everywhere, he is infused into us. To illustrate, think about the sun. It's fixed fast in the sky. Yet it's equally diffused over all countries. It's present everywhere. It's mingled and associated with all things. The same is true of God. He has made all things and sees all things. Nothing is secret from him. [Amos 9:2] He is present in the darkness, and in our innermost thoughts. Not only do we function in him, we *live* with him.

"We humans shouldn't flatter ourselves because of our numbers. We may seem many to ourselves, but to God we are very few. We divide ourselves into peoples and nations.

But to God this whole world is one family. Human kings need the reports of their civil servants in order to know what's happening in their kingdoms. But God has no need of reports. We live not only in his eyes, but in his bosom.

The Jews Suffer Because Of Disobedience.

"Still, you object, saying that it didn't benefit the Jews to worship this one God—even with altars, temples and great ceremony. The problem is that you're looking at later events with no knowledge of the earlier ones. As long as the Jews worshiped our God—indeed, the God of all mankind—with chastity, innocence, and pure religion, they grew from a few persons to an innumerable multitude. As long as they obeyed his wholesome laws, they changed from poor to rich, from servants to kings. A few overwhelmed many. Unarmed men conquered armed ones. Even the forces of nature fought on their behalf. [Ps. 78:44-53]

"Carefully read the Jews' own Scriptures and you will see that they deserve their present misfortune because of their own wickedness. [1 Chron. 9:1] If you prefer Roman writings, read about the Jews in the books of Flavius Josephus or Antoninus Julianus. Or read about them in ancient documents. You will see that nothing has happened to the Jews other than what had been foretold would happen if they continued in their course of obstinacy. You will then realize that they forsook God before they were forsaken by him. They were not taken into captivity along with their God, as you have claimed. Instead, they were abandoned by God because they abandoned his teachings.

Even The Philosophers Spoke Of The End Of The World.

"It's a foolish error to doubt that the earth will eventually be destroyed by fire. Even the heavens, with all the stars, will cease even as they began. The flow of the springs into the ocean, too, will eventually pass away into the power of fire. [2 Pet. 3:10] Who among your wise men doesn't acknowledge this? Who among them doubts that all things that have a beginning must also have an end, that all things which are made will eventually perish? For example, the Stoics have steadfastly taught that all the moisture of the earth will eventually be dried up and then the earth will catch fire. The Epicureans teach the same thing. Plato said that parts of the earth would alternately be inundated with water and then scorched with fire. Even though Plato said that the earth itself has been constructed indestructibly, he did acknowledge that God himself, its Creator, could destroy it.

We Believe In The Resurrection And Future Punishment.

"As you can see, the philosophers said many of the same things we are saying. But this isn't to say that we are copying them. Instead, they imitated the shadow of truth by taking from the divine announcements of the prophets. For example, two of the greatest thinkers, Plato and Pythagoras, taught a corrupted version of our doctrine of the resurrection of the dead. According to them, however, the physical body is forever dissolved, and the soul alone lives forever. They further corrupted the truth by saying that the souls of humans pass into new bodies, including those of cattle, birds, and beasts. Such an opinion is so absurd that it's worthy only of a clown, not a philosopher. Nevertheless, in the context of our argument, it's sufficient to note that even in the teaching of the resurrection, your wise men agree with us to a degree.

"But who is so foolish to deny that man, who could originally be formed by God, can also be re-formed by God? Who would deny that man was nothing before he began to exist and that he is nothing after death?* And that since it was possible for him to be formed from nothing, it's also possible for him to be restored from nothing? Obviously, it's more difficult to create something that has never been than to merely repeat something that has already existed.

*Although Octavius is probably referring only to the *body* here, not the soul, his remark might indicate that some early Christians believed that the soul was in a state of either non-existence or "soul-sleep" between death and the resurrection. If so, this would have been a minority view. *See* Tertullian *Treatise On the Soul*; Hippolytus *Against Plato*; Lactantius *Divine Institutes* 7.20.

"Do you think that simply because something is withdrawn from our feeble eyes, it perishes to God? Every body—whether it has returned to dust, dissolved in the sea, or changed into smoke and ashes—is withdrawn from us, but it is reserved for God. It has simply been placed, so to speak, in the custody of the natural elements. So we do not fear any loss from cremation, as you have charged. We simply adopt the ancient and better custom of burying in the earth.

"Notice how all of nature foreshadows a future resurrection. The sun sinks down, but then rises again. The stars pass away each morning, but then return. Flowers die, but they bloom again the next season. Trees lose their leaves in the autumn, but they return in the spring. Seeds do not flourish until they have decayed or been buried. [John 12:24] So a body in the grave is merely like the trees in winter, which appear to be dead. What hurry is there for the leaves to revive and return while it's still the dead of winter? Just as the trees must wait until spring, we must wait for the springtime of the body before its resurrection.

"Of course, I realize that many people prefer to believe that they will be nothing after death. Realizing the punishment they deserve, they would rather be altogether extinguished than to be restored for the purpose of punishment. And their wrongdoing is increased by the liberty granted them in this life and by God's very great patience. But the more tardy his judgment is, the much more just it is.

"In their writings, even your poets warn men about the fiery river that awaits them after death and the heat flowing from the Stygian marsh. These things have been prepared for their eternal torment and they were revealed to the poets by the demons and the oracles. So the poetic writings tell about Jupiter swearing religiously by the fiery banks and the black abyss. He shudders to think about the punishment that awaits him and his worshipers, for there is no measure or end to these torments. There, the intelligent fire burns the limbs and yet restores them. It both feeds on them and nourishes them. It's just like the fire of lightning bolts that strikes bodies and yet does not consume them. It's like the volcanic fires of Mt. Aetna and Mt. Vesuvius, which glow but are not wasted. Similarly, the fire of punishment is not fed by the waste of those who burn; it is nourished by the never-ending devouring of their bodies. [Rev. 14:9-11]

"But those who don't know God deserve to be tormented for their irreverence and unrighteousness. No one but a profane person hesitates to believe. It's no less wicked to be ignorant of the Parent and Lord of all than it is to offend him. Ignorance of God is sufficient for punishment, just as knowledge of him can bring pardon.

"If someone were to compare us Christians to you, he would find us to be much better than you. This is so even though your discipline is more severe in some regards. Although you forbid adultery, you still commit it. We, however, are men only for our own wives. You punish crimes when they're committed. With us, even to *think* of crimes is to sin. You're afraid of those who are aware of what you really do. We're afraid even of our own conscience, without which we cannot exist. Finally, the prisons spill over with people from your numbers. But there are no Christians there unless they have been imprisoned because of their faith, or else they are apostates from their faith.

Fate Is Simply God's Foreknowledge.

"No one should either take comfort from or apologize for what happens from fate. Even if what happens is the arrangement of fortune, the mind is still free. So a man's actions, not his position, are judged. For what else is fate other than what God has spoken about each one of us? Since he can foresee our make-up, he can also determine our fate, according to the just deserts and qualities of each individual. We are not punished because of the star under which we are born, but because of our disposition and nature. I think that's enough said about fate. If I have not explained our position on fate sufficiently, we can address that matter more fully at another time."*

---

*As he himself indicates, Octavius has really not fully explained the early Christian view on fate and predestination. The *First Apology* of Justin Martyr, which follows, explains the early Christian view in more detail.

9

Martyrdom, Poverty, And Holiness

Octavius continued his defense: "That many of us are called poor is not our disgrace, but our glory. As our mind is relaxed by luxury, it's strengthened by poverty. Yet who can be poor if he does not want, if he does not crave the possessions of others? Who can be poor if he is rich toward God? [Rev. 2:9; Matt. 6:19,20] Rather, he is poor who, having much, craves still more.

"Birds live without any estate. The cattle are fed each day. Yet these creatures are born for us. We possess all these things—that is, if we don't lust after them. A traveler is happier the lighter his load. Likewise, we are happier on this journey of life when we walk in poverty, rather than groaning under the heavy burden of riches.

"Yet, even if we thought that wealth were useful to us, we would ask for it from God. Since all wealth is ultimately his, he could distribute some of it to us if he wanted. But we would rather despise riches than to strive for them. We would rather possess innocence than wealth. We prefer to ask God for patience rather than for riches. We would rather be good than extravagant.

We Are Not Afraid To Die!

"You think we're being punished when we suffer hardships and infirmities. But it's not punishment—it's warfare. Fortitude is strengthened by infirmities. [Jas. 1:12] Virtue and suffering usually go hand in hand. Both the body and the mind grow sluggish without hard work. Think of all the mighty men you hold up as an example. Wasn't it their afflictions that made them great? God is not unable to aid us, as you have claimed, nor does he despise us. He loves his own people, and he is the ruler of all men. However, he tests us and searches us through adversities. He tests the qualities of all of us through trials, often even to death itself. He can test us to the point of death because he knows that nothing can perish to him. Just as gold is refined by the fire, so are we proven through times of crisis. [Mal. 3:3]

> *We are happier on this journey of life when we walk in poverty.*

"It's a beautiful spectacle to God when a Christian battles pain—or when he stands up to threats, punishment, and torture. When he mocks both the horrors of the executioner and the roar of the crowd screaming for his death. When he stands up to kings and princes as a free man, yielding only to God, to whom he belongs. And when he is triumphant and victorious, he tramples on the very man who has pronounced his death sentence. For the one who obtains the prize for which he has contended—he is the conqueror. [Rev. 2:10,11]

"What soldier, when under the eyes of his general, would not incur peril with greater boldness? No one receives a reward before his trial. Yet a general can't give what is beyond his power. He can't give life to the soldier. He can only bestow glory and honor for the warfare. In contrast, God's soldier is neither forsaken in his suffering nor is he brought to an end by death. So although you think we

Christians must be miserable, we are not at all. [Matt.5:11,12; 10:28]

"You praise to the skies the sufferings of your brave men. Take Mucius Scaevola, for example. When his attempt to kill the invading king failed, he bravely sacrificed his right hand in the fire. And his life was spared because of his heroism. Yet look at how many of our people have not only allowed their right hands to be burned, but their whole bodies as well. And they have endured this without any cries of pain, even though it was in their power to avoid this punishment [by simply renouncing Christ]. And I'm not just comparing our *men* with Mucius Scaevola. For even our boys and young women treat your crosses, tortures, wild beasts, and other horrors with contempt and patient suffering. Don't you realize that *nobody* is willing to endure such punishment without a reason? That nobody is able to endure such tortures without help from God?

Christians Prefer Poverty.

"Maybe you haven't noticed, but those who do not know God are rich, powerful and lavished with honors. [1 Tim. 6:9,10] Miserable men! They are lifted up higher merely to fall lower in the end. They're like cattle fattened before the slaughter. [Jas.5:5] Or the sacrificial animals who are decorated right before they're killed. Some are given empires and dominions so that their unlimited power will give them the opportunity for the unbridled immorality that is characteristic of ruined souls. Since death is inevitable for everyone, what true happiness can there be apart from the knowledge of God? Like a dream, happiness slips away before it is grasped.

> *What good does it do to glitter in purple and yet be filthy in mind?*

"Are you a king? Yet you fear others as much as you are feared. You may be surrounded by abundant followers, yet you are alone in the presence of danger. Are you rich? Yet trusting in wealth is folly. The brief journey of life is not made easier by a large amount of traveling baggage—it's made harder. Do you wear the robes and carry the staff of a magistrate? But what good does it do to glitter in purple and yet be filthy in your mind? It's simply vanity and empty worship of social rank. Are you of noble birth? Do you praise your lineage? Yet we are still all born with one lot. We are distinguished in life only by virtue. [Jas. 2:1-9]

We Shun The World's Entertainment.

"So among ourselves, we honor others for their character and modesty. For that reason, we abstain from evil pleasures and from your splendors and public games. [1 Pet. 4:3,4] We condemn these enticements, knowing from sacred things their origin. We shudder from the madness of the crowds brawling among themselves at the chariot games and from the teaching of murder in the gladiatorial contests. The madness is no less at your dramas. Instead, the debauchery is more prolonged. Sometimes an actor expounds on adultery; other times he acts it out. Another actor may entice the audience to lust. The same actor insults your gods by attributing to them adulteries and feuds. Another actor brings you to tears when he plays the part of one suffering or dying. How strange! You demand actual murder in the arena, but then you weep at fictitious murder in your plays.

We Avoid Even The Appearance Of Idol Worship.

"Yes, we despise things sacrificed to your gods, as well as the cups out of which drink offerings have been poured. [Acts. 15:28,29] But this isn't a confession of fear. Rather, it's an assertion of true liberty. We realize that the things God has created as gifts for us can't be corrupted by the agency of another. But we abstain from these things so that no one will think that we're submitting ourselves to the demons to which the sacrifice was made. [1 Cor. 10:18-21] We also don't want anyone to think that we are ashamed of our own religion.

"As for wearing flowers, who doesn't know how much we indulge ourselves in the flowers of spring? We gather roses, lilies, and whatever other flowers are beautiful and fragrant. We not only use individual flowers for various purposes, we even wear garlands of them around our necks. Please excuse us, however, for not wearing crowns of flowers on our heads. We prefer to breathe in the sweet fragrance of flowers through our nostrils—not through the back of our heads!*

"Nor do we crown the dead. I have to wonder at you for lavishing garlands of flowers on a dead body—a body that can't smell them. If the dead person is blessed, he doesn't need flowers. If he is in misery, he takes no delight in flowers. We adorn our funeral rites with the same tranquility with which we live. We don't tie a withering garland to our dead bodies. Instead, we wear a garland made with eternal flowers from God. We are secure in the generosity of our God. The confidence of his present majesty animates our hope of future joy. Not only will we rise again, we are already living in contemplation of the future.

"So let Socrates, the Athenian buffoon, confess that he knows nothing about God, if he wants to! Let Simonides postpone forever his opinion about God! Let all the philosophers of the Greek Academy deliberate! We despise the bent brows of the philosophers. We know them to be corrupters, adulterers, and tyrants; yet, they are ever eloquent against their own vices. We carry our wisdom in our minds— not in our robes.

> *We don't speak great things—we live them.*

We don't speak great things—we live them! We can boast that we have attained what the philosophers so earnestly sought for, but were never able to find.

"Yes, in our time, the truth about God has finally ripened. But why be unhappy about it? This is the time to rejoice! Let

---

*The early Christians did not follow the pagan practice of crowning their heads with wreaths made of flowers or foliage, since this practice had originated from pagan worship festivities. *See* Tertullian *The Crown*.

superstition be overthrown. Let ungodliness be destroyed. And let true religion prevail!"

Caecilius Speaks Up.

When Octavius concluded his speech, we both sat stunned in silence for awhile, our faces rapt with attention. I was filled with admiration for my friend Octavius because he had expressed so beautifully the things that are easier to feel than to say. He had defended Christianity with arguments, examples, and written authorities. He had repelled his opponent's attack by using the very weapons with which the attacker had armed himself—the sayings of the philosophers. Octavius had shown that the truth is not only simple, but quite wonderful. While I was ruminating on these things, Caecilius suddenly broke the silence: "Well, I don't have to wait for your decision, Mark. The victory is clearly mine!"

I was surprised by what he said.† "I can't believe *he's* claiming the victory," I thought to myself.†

"Yes, I'm the victor," he continued, "even though I've been conquered. For I've been conquered by truth, and now I'm triumphant over error. I now confess the truth about the Creator, and I yield to God. I see the truth about your way of life—which is now my way of life. However, I still have many questions. It's not that I'm still resisting the truth, but rather that I want my training to be complete. But the sun is setting now, so why don't we meet again tomorrow and discuss these things in more detail."

Standing up, I now spoke: "As for myself, I rejoice on behalf of all of us. I'm glad that the task of judging has been taken from me. Although I can praise Octavius for the merit of his words, the praises of men are weak. His real reward is from God, who enabled him to gain the victory."

And so we ambled back to the village, smiling and rejoicing. Caecilius rejoiced that he now believed. Octavius rejoiced that he had been able to effectively present the truth to Caecilius. And I—I was happy both that the one had believed and the other had conquered.

Part Two

The First Apology of
Justin Martyr

Justin Martyr: Philosopher Turned Evangelist

A few decades after the Apostle John's death, a young philosopher named Justin embarked on a spiritual journey to find truth. One day, while he was walking to his accustomed place of meditation in a secluded field overlooking the Mediterranean, he noticed an old man walking at a distance behind him. Wanting to be left alone, he turned and stared with annoyance at the elderly man. However, the old man, who turned out to be a Christian, struck up a conversation and learned that Justin was a philosopher. The old man then began to ask some soul-searching questions, helping Justin to see the deficiency of human philosophy.

As Justin later reminisced, "When the old man had spoken these and many other things, he left, encouraging me to think about what he had said. I've never seen him since, but immediately a flame was kindled in my soul. I was overwhelmed by a love for the prophets and the friends of Christ. After pondering over the things the old man had said, I realized that Christianity was the only true and worthwhile philosophy."*

After becoming a Christian, Justin continued to wear his philosopher's robe to symbolize that he had found the one true philosophy. He eventually became an evangelist, bringing many Romans—learned and unlearned alike—to conversion. During Justin's entire Christian life, Christianity was an outlawed religion. Justin realized, however, that much of the persecution resulted from false rumors about Christians. He felt that if the government knew the truth about Christians,

---

*Justin *Conversation with Trypho* 8.

it might halt its savage persecution. So at the risk of his own life, Justin penned the following apology, addressing it to Emperor Antoninus Pius. In the end, Justin's witness for Christ did cost him his life. A group of philosophers plotting against him had him arrested and sentenced to death. Choosing to die rather than to denounce Christ, Justin was executed in about 165 A.D. After his death, he became known as Justin the Martyr, or simply Justin Martyr.

Apart from the inspired New Testament writings, the subject apology is perhaps the single most valuable work of early Christianity. It furnishes detailed descriptions of church services, baptism, and the Lord's Supper. These descriptions are among the earliest we have. The value of this apology is enhanced by the fact that it was not written by some "church father" trying to tell the church what to teach or how to conduct its worship services. Instead, it was simply written by an evangelist explaining to the Romans what Christians believed and how they conducted their meetings. Throughout his work, Justin repeatedly uses the expression, "We have been taught... ." He was not the teacher; he was simply relating what he and other Christians had been taught.

Justin Knew Scripture

One of the more impressive things about Justin is his thorough knowledge of Scripture. In this apology alone, Justin quotes more than 155 Bible verses. That may not seem very remarkable, except that he quotes entirely *from memory*. Justin's grasp of the Bible is almost unbelievable. In his apology, he deftly rattles off prophecy after prophecy from the Old Testament. Even though quoting from memory, he nearly always attributes these prophecies to the correct persons, and many of his quotations follow almost verbatim the Greek Septuagint text, the standard translation used by the early Christians. Of course, since he wrote entirely from memory, Justin occasionally attributes a verse to the wrong prophet or makes a minor historical error. For example, he refers to Jethro as being Moses' uncle instead of his father-in-law. Yet such errors are remarkably few.

Philosophy And The Logos

In order to fully appreciate Justin's arguments, you will need to understand the significance of two Greek words he uses repeatedly throughout his apology: *philosophia* and *logos*. *Philosophia* (philosophy) simply means "love of wisdom." So when Justin tells the rulers they should make a decision based on philosophy, he is not referring to some school of thought. Instead, he means that the rulers' decision about Christians should be based on love of wisdom, not on hearsay or fear of the crowds.

Justin also frequently uses the word *logos*. The New Testament writers use this same word many times. For example, the Apostle John opened his Gospel with the well-known words: "In the beginning was the Word [Logos] and the Word [Logos] was with God. And the Word [Logos] was God" (John 1:1). Although our English Bibles generally translate *logos* with the term "word," *logos* also means "reason." When John writes that Jesus was the Logos of God, most of his readers probably understood him to say that Jesus is the Reason of God. In other words, Jesus is the embodiment of God's all-pervasive, rational power.

The early Christians recognized that God is the source of all reason and knowledge. So they believed that any *reasonable* person would want to serve the Reason (Logos) of God. Justin emphasizes this theme throughout his work. Like so many other early Christians, Justin saw no conflict between reason and his religion. To him, the two were inseparable.

1

We Want You To Investigate Us

To the Emperor Antoninus Pius, and to his adopted sons, Marcus Aurelius Verus and Lucius Verus, the philosophers. Also to the venerable Senate, and to all the people of Rome.

I, Justin, the son of Priscus, a native of Flavia Neapolis in Palestine, present this address and petition on behalf of a certain group of persons of all nations who are unjustly hated and cruelly abused. They are called Christians.† And I myself am one of them.

Reason dictates that persons who are truly noble and who love wisdom will honor and love only what is true. They will refuse to follow traditional viewpoints if those viewpoints are worthless. In fact, reason dictates that we should reject the opinions of those persons who did or taught anything wrong. Instead, a person who genuinely loves truth must choose to do and speak what is true, even if he is threatened with death. Since you are deemed to be noble persons, true philosophers, guardians of justice and lovers of truth, please listen to what I'm about to tell you. Your true character will be revealed by your response.

I have not come to flatter you by this written petition, nor to impress you by my words. I have come simply to beg that you do not pass judgment until you have made an accurate and thorough investigation. Your investigation must be free of prejudice, hearsay, and any desire to simply please the superstitious crowds. As for us, we are convinced that you can inflict no lasting evil on us. We can only do it to ourselves by proving to be wicked people. You can kill us—but you cannot harm us. [Matt. 10:28]

So that no one thinks I am writing recklessly, we not only request that the charges against us Christians be investigated, we *demand* it. If anyone can prove that the charges they make against us are true, then punish us as we deserve. But if no one can convict Christians of anything wrong, justice forbids you to punish innocent people simply because of false rumors. In fact, any reasonable person will recognize that the only fair and just solution is that we Christians render an account of our own lives and doctrines. After hearing us out, then make your decision based on justice and philosophy, not on mob violence.

In short, it is our responsibility as Christians to bare ourselves before you—to enable all of you to inspect our lives and teachings. If we fail to do so, we will be guilty for not making our real teachings and practices known to all. On the other hand, it is your responsibility, once you have heard us out, to prove to be good judges. For if after you have learned the truth, you still do not do what is just, you will stand before God without excuse.

What's In A Name?

The mere application of a name doesn't prove anything— either good or bad. It is wrong, therefore, to convict us as criminals merely because of our name. Instead, once you ascertain that we have committed no wrong, it is your responsibility to earnestly *protect* us from being unjustly punished. You will thereby protect yourselves from incurring just punishment from God. A mere name deserves neither praise nor punishment by itself. Rather, you must first prove that either praiseworthy or evil actions have been committed by those bearing the name.

You do not punish any *other* accused persons unless they are first convicted of wrongdoing. It is only in our case that you accept our name as sufficient evidence by itself to punish us. If a person acknowledges that he is a Christian, you punish him merely on the basis of his acknowledgment. On the other hand, if an accused Christian simply denies that he is a Christian, you acquit him. You accept his mere denial as evidence that he is not a criminal. But justice requires that you look into the life and actions of both the one who confesses and the one who denies. His deeds will make it apparent what type of person he is.

Since you are a philosopher, you can readily see how this same principle applies to persons who call themselves philosophers. Many take the name "philosopher" and wear philosopher's robes, but they are altogether unworthy of the name. In fact, the opinions and teachings of the ancient philosophers were quite diverse. Some of them even promoted atheism. Today, the poet philosophers teach that Jupiter committed incest with his own children. Yet you do not punish them for teaching such things. Instead, you lavish prizes and honors on them.

2

Christians Are No Threat To The Empire

When you hear that we seek a kingdom, you suppose—without making any inquiry—that we speak of a human kingdom. But that is not so. We are speaking of a kingdom that is with God. [John 18:36] That is why we so openly confess our faith when charged with being Christians, even though we know that death is the punishment for our confession. If we were looking for a human kingdom, we would simply deny our Christ in order to escape death. We would do our utmost to conceal the fact that we are Christians, so that we might live to attain such a human kingdom. But since our thoughts are not fixed on the present, we are not concerned when men kill us. We recognize that death is a debt that we must eventually pay anyway.

Christians Are Your Allies

Please understand that Christians are your allies. For one thing, we help to promote peace and order. For example, we teach that it is impossible for anyone—the wicked or virtuous—to escape God's notice. We teach that every person will eventually receive everlasting punishment or everlasting salvation, according to the merits of his actions. [Matt. 25:31-46; John 5:28] If everyone believed this, no one would choose wickedness even for a short time, realizing that he would receive the punishment of everlasting fire. Everyone would restrain himself and clothe himself with righteousness so he would obtain the good gifts of God and escape his punishments.

It's not the same, however, with human laws. Even though you impose laws and punish those who break them, people still commit crimes. That is because they know you are merely men and that it's quite possible to escape detection. However, if those same persons were convinced that nothing they did—in fact, nothing they even *intended*—could escape God's detection, they would by all means live virtuous lives in order to escape punishment. I think you will admit this yourselves.

So you should be grateful for the message that Christians preach—unless, that is, you are afraid that all men will become righteous and you will no longer have anyone to punish. While that may be of concern to public executioners, surely that is not your concern. Undoubtedly, you who seek virtue and wisdom will not act unreasonably. Still, that is your choice. If you would rather join the ranks of the foolish, and to prize public opinion more than truth, then do whatever you have power to do. But rulers who value public opinion more than truth are no better than the robbers who rule over the desert wastelands. And the Logos himself declares that you will not succeed if you follow such a course of action. And we know that there is no ruler more kingly or just than he, other than the God from whom he was begotten. And a reasonable person will not choose the things that the Logos [Reason] condemns. Our teacher, Jesus Christ, foretold many things that would come to pass. And he is both the Son and the Apostle of God,* who is the Father and Ruler of all. It is from this Jesus Christ that we have taken the name Christians. Actually, our confidence in his teachings grows daily because we are eyewitnesses to the fact that the things he told us beforehand have come to pass. Surely it is the work

---

*The word "apostle" means "one who is sent forth." Jesus is the Apostle of God in the sense of having been sent from God. (John 17:3)

of God when someone prophesies and then things happen just as he said they would.

So that you can fully understand who we are, I'm going to briefly explain how we live and what our Master Jesus taught.[†] Please understand that it is for your own sake that I'm explaining these things. Don't you realize that it is in our power, when we are brought to trial, to simply deny that we are Christians? But we would rather die than to live by telling a lie. We earnestly seek the life that is eternal and pure. We yearn for a home with God, the Father and Creator of all. We confess our faith without shame because we are convinced that those who long to live with God in the place where there is no sin can obtain our hope. But we must prove to God by our works that we have followed him. This is what Christ taught, what we believe, and what we teach.

Yet, I am going to forewarn you to be on your guard so that the demons will not deceive you. They will try to divert you from reading and understanding what I'm saying. They want to keep you as their slaves and servants. Sometimes they appear in dreams; other times, in magical rites. By those means, they enslave all who do not seek salvation by actively opposing them. For that reason, ever since our conversion to serve the Logos, we keep free from demons and follow the only Unbegotten God through his Son.

Since it is in your power to investigate us thoroughly, please examine us to verify that the things I'm about to tell you are truly the teachings that Christ himself gave us and are truly the principles we continue to teach.

3

What Christians Believe And Practice

The teachings of Jesus have transformed our lives.[†] We who previously delighted in immorality now embrace chastity exclusively. We who used to practice magical arts now devote our lives to the Good and Unbegotten God. We who valued the acquisition of wealth and possessions above all things now bring what we have into a common pool and share with everyone in need. [Acts 4:32] Many of us used to hate and destroy one another; we would not live with people of a different race because of their different customs. But now, since the coming of Christ, we live familiarly with such people, and we pray for our enemies. We seek to persuade those who unjustly hate us to live by the wonderful teachings of Christ so that they can enjoy the wonderful hope of God's reward with us.

What Jesus Taught

The teachings of Christ were brief and concise. He was not skilled in devious argumentation, but rather his word was the power of God.

Chastity

Concerning chastity, he taught us:

- "Whoever looks upon a woman with lust has already committed adultery with her in his heart before God" [Matt. 5:28].
- "If your right eye offends you, cut it out. For it is better for you to enter into the kingdom of heaven with one eye than to be cast into everlasting fire with two eyes" [Matt. 5:29].
- "Whoever marries a woman who is divorced from another husband commits adultery" [Matt. 5:32].
- "There are some who have been made eunuchs by men and some who were born eunuchs. There are also those who have made themselves eunuchs for the kingdom of heaven's sake. But all cannot receive this saying" [Matt. 19:12].

In other words, anyone who is married twice by human law is a sinner in the eyes of our Master.* And so is anyone who looks upon a woman with lust. For Christ not only rejects those who commit adultery in deed, but also those who *desire* to commit adultery. For not only are our *works* open before God, but also our *thoughts*.

Many men and women who have been Christ's disciples since childhood are still chaste virgins at the age of 60 or 70. In fact, I can produce examples of such Christians from every race of mankind. Not only that, but there are countless multitudes of those who used to live in debauchery but have now changed their lustful habits and accepted these teachings. For Christ did not call merely the just and chaste to repentance, but also the ungodly and immoral. In fact, he said, "I came to call, not the righteous, but sinners to repentance" [Matt. 9:13]. The heavenly Father does not wish to punish sinners; he would rather have them repent.

---

*It is generally assumed that Justin is referring only to remarriage after divorce, or perhaps to remarriage after divorce other than for adultery.

We have also been taught that to abandon newborn infants is utterly wicked. So we do not join you in this practice, in order to avoid doing injury to anyone and to avoid sinning against God. We realize that most abandoned infants—both girls and boys—are brought up for prostitution. They are reared for this shameful purpose the same as shepherds raise herds of sheep or goats. And because of this, multitudes of prostitutes are found in every nation. Although you should outlaw prostitution, you collect tax revenue from it instead. Because abandoning children is so commonly practiced, anyone lying with a prostitute may well be having sexual relations with his own child, his own sister or his own brother.

Furthermore, some people hire out their own children or wives as prostitutes. Some boys are even purposefully mutilated for sodomy. In fact, prostitution is often performed as a mystery rite to "the Mother of the gods." How ironic that you accuse us of all sorts of debauched practices, when the truth is that it is *you* who do these very things openly. And you applaud them. You act as though the divine lamp itself were overturned and extinguished. Since we are innocent of these charges, it does not defile us for people to falsely accuse us of such things. However, those who practice such lewd acts and then falsely accuse us are doing great harm to themselves.

> *Although you should outlaw prostitution, you collect tax revenue from it instead.*

Another reason we refuse to abandon newborn babies is out of fear that they might not be picked up. If they were to die, we would be guilty of murder. So when we marry, it is only so that we might raise children. And those of us who remain single live in chastity. Therefore, promiscuous sexual relations are certainly not one of our mystery rites. In fact, not too long ago, one of our young men tried to hire a surgeon to make him into a eunuch. However, the surgeon told the young man that he would have to have permission from the

governor to do such a thing. So the young Christian then
petitioned Felix, the governor of Alexandria, for permission.
When Felix denied his petition, he chose to remain single and
chaste anyway, satisfied in his mind that he had done all that
he could in this regard. He also had the approval of others of
like mind.*

Love Toward All People/ Material Riches

Concerning the love that we are to have toward all people,
Christ taught:

- "If you love only those who love you, what new thing
  have you done? Even the ungodly do this. But I say
  unto you, 'Pray for your enemies and love those who
  hate you. Bless those who curse you, and pray for those
  who mistreat you'" [Matt. 5:46,44].

- He also taught that we should share with the needy
  and do nothing for personal glory, saying, "Give to
  him that asks, and do not turn away the one who
  wishes to borrow. If you only lend to those from whom
  you expect to receive, what new thing have you done?
  Even the tax collectors do this" [Matt. 5:42,46].

- "Do not lay up for yourselves treasure upon earth,
  where moth and rust consume. For what does it profit
  a man to gain the whole world if he loses his own soul?
  Or what shall a man give in exchange for his soul? Lay
  up treasure, therefore, in heaven, where neither moth
  nor rust consume" [Matt. 6:19, 16:26, 6:20].

- "Be kind and merciful, just as your Father is kind and
  merciful. He makes his sun rise on the righteous and
  the wicked alike. Take no thought of what you will eat,
  or what you will put on. Are you not worth more than
  the birds and the animals? Yet God feeds them. So do
  not worry about what you will eat or what you will
  put on. For your heavenly Father knows that you need

*As Octavius pointed out, the church in general understood Jesus to be
speaking figuratively in Matt. 19:12. Although a few early Christians did take
Jesus' words literally, this was not the normal practice of the church.

all these things. But seek the kingdom of heaven, and all these things will be added unto you. For where a man's treasure is, there his mind is also" [Matt. 5:45; 6:25,26, 33,21].

- Finally, he taught us, "Do not do these things in order to be seen by men. Otherwise, you will have no reward from your Father in heaven" [Matt. 6:1].

Nonresistance

Christ also taught us to suffer patiently, to be ready to serve all others, and to be free from anger. "If a man strikes you on one cheek, offer the other to him also. And do not hinder the one who would take away your cloak or coat. Whoever stays angry is in danger of the fire of punishment. If anyone compels you to go with him a mile, go two. And let your good works shine before men that, upon seeing them, they may glorify your Father in heaven" [Luke 6:29; Matt. 5:22,41,16].

Christ also taught us not to struggle with others, or to imitate wicked people. Rather, he urged us to lead all people away from dishonor and wickedness by our patience and gentleness. The fact that we actually follow his teachings is demonstrated by the many Christians who once followed your way of thinking. Now they have changed their violent and oppressive dispositions. Some of them were won to Christianity by the righteousness they observed in the life of their Christian neighbors. Others were won by the extraordinary restraint Christian travelers displayed when they were cheated. Still others were attracted by the honesty of the Christians with whom they transacted business.

Swearing

Christ also taught us to not swear at all, but rather to always speak the truth, commanding us: "Swear not at all. Rather, let your 'yes' mean yes; and your 'no,' no. For whatever you add beyond this comes from evil" [Matt. 5:34,37].

Worship God Alone

He also taught us to worship God alone, saying, "The greatest commandment is, 'You shall worship the Lord your God.' And you should serve only the Lord God who created you, with all your heart and with all your strength" [Mark 12:30]. In fact, when a certain man came to him and addressed him as "Good Master," he replied, "There is no one good but God alone, who made all things" [Matt. 19:16,17].

Taxes

More so than the rest of your subjects, we Christians endeavor to always pay the taxes you demand, including the special assessments you occasionally make. For Christ taught us to do this. When certain men came to him and asked him if it was proper to pay taxes to Caesar, he replied, "'Tell me, whose image is on the coin?' They answered, 'Caesar's.' He then told them, 'Therefore, give to Caesar the things that are Caesar's, but give to God the things that are God's" [Matt. 22:17,19-21]. For that reason, we give worship to God alone. In other things, however, we gladly serve you, acknowledging you as our kings and rulers. And we pray that you will exercise sound judgment with your kingly power.

False Christians

Someone may say, "We know of some Christians who have been arrested and proven to be lawbreakers." But is it right to condemn all of us because of what some individuals have done? Those who are, in fact, truly criminals are not the ones I am describing. Just as all sorts of Greeks are called philosophers, so all sorts of barbarians are called Christians. That's why it's so important for you to examine the deeds of those who are accused before you. If someone is truly a criminal, let him be punished as a *criminal*, not as a *Christian*. But if a person has done no wrong, he should be acquitted.

The fact that a person is a Christian does not of itself make him a criminal. However, even though we are falsely accused, we do not ask that you punish the persons who falsely accuse us. Their own wickedness and ignorance of what is right is sufficient punishment.

Let it be understood that those who are not living by Christ's teachings are not Christians at all—even though they might profess his teachings with their lips. For Christ himself said that it is not the ones who merely make a profession of him who will be saved, but the ones *who do the works*, warning "Not everyone who says to me, 'Lord, Lord,' shall enter into the kingdom of heaven, but he who does the will of my Father who is in heaven. For whoever listens to me and follows my teachings listens to him who sent me. For many will say unto me, 'Lord, Lord, did we not eat and drink in your name, and perform wonders in it?' But then I will say to them, 'Depart from me you workers of evil.' Then there will be weeping and gnashing of teeth when the wicked are sent into everlasting fire. But the righteous will shine as the sun. Remember that many will come in my name, covered in sheep's clothing, although they are actually ravenous wolves inside. By their works you will know them. Every tree that does not produce good fruit will be cut down and cast into the fire" [Matt. 7:21-23; Matt. 13:42,43; 7:15,16,19]. In fact, those who are not living by Christ's teachings, but are Christians in name only, we *expect* you to punish for whatever wrong they have done.

> *Let it be understood that those who are not living by Christ's teachings are not Christians at all.*

I could end my defense at this point, simply demanding that we receive what is just and true. However, I appreciate the fact that it's not easy to change one's thinking, particularly concerning something he knows little about. Therefore, for those of you who love the truth, I want to explain more about us.

4

Rewards And Punishments After Death

Even if you ignore our pleas and disregard our frank explanations, we will suffer no permanent loss. For we are persuaded that every man will suffer punishment in eternal fire according to the merits of his deeds. [Matt. 25:41-46] We also believe that every person will offer an account for the power he has received from God. For Christ said, "To whom God has given more, more shall be required of him" [Luke 12:48].

Think for a moment about the rulers who preceded you. They all died, the same as other men. If death meant the end of all sensation, it would be a blessing to the wicked. However, sensation does not end with death. Rather, eternal punishment is stored up for the wicked after they die. [Rev. 20:10; 21:8] Therefore, do not be slow to accept the things I am telling you.

Yet if you don't believe me, listen to your own oracles, Magi, and spiritists. They will tell you that souls retain sensation after death. In fact, these spiritists try to communicate with the departed souls of humans. They even slaughter innocent children in order to learn the future and secret things from their souls. You are well aware that some persons, whom you call demon-possessed and maniacs, are seized by the spirits of the dead and are cast about by them. Listen to your own oracles. Listen to your philosophers— men like Pythagoras, Plato, and Socrates. Take note of the poet Homer, who wrote that Ulysses inquired of the souls of the dead.

Since you respect the views of such people, show the same respect for our beliefs. We certainly hold a firmer belief in God than they did. For we expect to obtain our own bodies back again, even though we may die and be buried. [John 5:28,29] Though this may sound impossible to you, we are convinced that nothing is impossible with God. [Luke 1:37]

The Resurrection Is Not Impossible

If you are convinced that bodily resurrection from the dead is impossible, think for a moment about human reproduction itself. Suppose you came from another world and someone showed you a small drop of human seed. Then he showed you a picture of a man. Finally, he told you confidently that the small drop you were seeing would produce a man as pictured. You would probably say it was impossible.

The resurrection of the dead is much the same.[†] You think that it's impossible for the dead to rise again because you have never seen it happen. But just as a small drop of seed can produce a full grown human being, so likewise our decayed bodies, which are buried in the earth like seed, can rise again in God's due time to a state of incorruption. People who say that such a thing is impossible even for God himself are rather short-sighted. I wonder if they believe that they themselves were produced from a small seed.

We have learned that it is better to have faith in things that might seem impossible than to be unbelieving like the rest of the world. Our Master Jesus Christ said, "What is impossible with men is possible with God" [Matt. 19:26]. He also said, "Do not fear those who kill you, but after that can do no more. But fear him who after death is able to cast both soul and body into Gehenna" [Matt. 10:28]. And Gehenna is a place of punishment for those who live wickedly and for those who do not believe all these things that God taught us through Christ.

The demons cannot keep hidden the fact that there will be a fire for the punishment of the wicked. For they have been unable to keep the name of Christ hidden. All they can do is to cause us to be hated and killed by persons who live without reason [*logos*], who live immorally in wicked customs, and who are bigoted. However, we do not hate those people. Rather, as our conduct shows, we sympathize with them and try to help them repent. As I have said before, we do not fear death. Everyone eventually dies anyway. And there is nothing new under the sun, but all things continue the same in the order of the world. [Eccl. 1:9]

Those who are not satisfied with the things of this world should pay attention to our teachings. For through them, they can live eternally, free from both suffering and want. Yet if they believe that there is nothing after death—that those who die pass into insensibility—then they are our benefactors when they set us free from the sufferings and burdens of this life. But they only prove themselves to be wicked, inhuman, and bigoted. For their purpose in killing us is not to deliver us, but rather to cut us off from life and pleasure.

> *The paintings of your gods usually depict a serpent along with the gods.*

Significance Of The Serpent

We notice that the paintings of your gods usually depict a serpent along with the gods. To you, the serpent is a symbol of great mystery. As for us, we call the prince of the demons "the serpent." You can verify this by examining our writings. We say that this serpent, whom we also call "Satan" and "the devil," will be sent into the fire of eternal punishment along with his host of demons and the humans who follow him. The only reason that this punishment has been delayed is because of God's love for mankind. [2 Pet. 3:9] He knows in advance that some people will be saved through repentance. [Acts 13:48] Some of these people have not yet even been born.

In the beginning, God created man with the power to reason and the ability to choose to do what is right and true. [Gen. 2:16,17] So all men are without excuse before God, since they are born with the ability to reason and to observe. If anyone refuses to believe that God is concerned about the state of affairs here on earth, he in effect says that God delights in wickedness. Or that God is like an unfeeling stone. Or that notions of good and evil exist only in the minds of people. Or, ultimately, that God doesn't even exist. But to assert any of these things is the greatest profanity.

But even if you say that our views are absurd or impossible, that is our business. Our views do not harm anyone else—as long as you cannot convict us of any wrongdoing.

5

How A Person Can Be Born Again

So that you will fully understand everything there is to know about us, I want to describe the manner in which we dedicate ourselves to God when we have been made new through Christ. First, those persons who are convinced that what we teach is true, and who promise that they can live accordingly, are instructed to implore God with prayer and fasting for the forgiveness of all past sins. We pray and fast with them. Then we take them to a place where there is water, and they are spiritually reborn in the same manner in which we ourselves were reborn. Then they are washed with water in the name of God, the Father and Lord of the universe, and of our Saviour Jesus Christ, and of the Holy Spirit. [Matt. 28:19] For Christ said, "Unless you are born again, you will not enter into the kingdom of heaven" [John 3:5].*

Of course, it is obvious that it's impossible for a person who has already been born to re-enter his mother's womb. Rather, Isaiah the prophet explained how those who have sinned, but are repentant, can escape their sins: "'Wash and

---

*It seems to have been a universal understanding of the early church that Jesus was referring to water baptism in his words to Nicodemus. See Irenaeus *Fragments from Lost Writings*, no. 34; Clement *Instructor* 1. 6; Cyprian *To Donatus* 3. However, as Justin also made clear, personal faith and heartfelt repentance preceded baptism. A person without faith was not reborn merely by going through the motions of water baptism.

be clean. Put all evil away from your souls. Learn to do what is right. Help the fatherless and plead for the widow. And come and let us reason together,' says the Lord. 'And though your sins may be as scarlet, I will make them white as wool. Though they may be crimson, I will make them white as snow'" [Isa. 1:16-20].

The apostles taught us the reason for this ceremony, as follows. We have no say in our original birth. It results from the union of our parents. And often we grow up ignorant of the truth, being raised in bad habits and being taught wicked things. However, we do not have to remain the children of necessity and ignorance. We can become the children of choice and knowledge through a second birth. [Titus 3:5]

In order for a person to obtain the forgiveness of his past sins in the water, there is pronounced over him—the one choosing to be born again and who has repented of his sins—the name of God, the Father and Lord of the universe. [Acts 2:38; 22:16] The man who leads the candidate to the place of washing refers to God only by that designation. For no one can utter the name of the inexpressible God. In fact, if anyone dares to say that there is such a name, he raves with a hopeless madness.

This washing is called illumination because those who learn these things are illuminated in their understanding. And the person to be illuminated is washed also in the name of Jesus Christ, who was crucified under Pontius Pilate, and in the name of the Holy Spirit.

6

What We Do At Our Weekly Meetings

After we have washed the one who has been convinced and who has accepted our teaching, we bring him to the place where those who are called brothers are assembled. There we offer heartfelt prayers for both ourselves and the baptized person. We also pray for everyone else in every place. We pray that, now that we have learned the truth, we may be counted worthy by our works to be found good citizens and keepers of the commandments, so that we may be saved with an everlasting salvation. [Matt. 7:21-23] When we are finished praying, we greet each other with a kiss.[1] Then bread and a cup of wine mixed with water are brought to the presiding brother.[2] Upon taking them, he gives praise and glory to the Father of the universe, through the name of the Son and of the Holy Spirit. And he gives thanks at considerable length for our being counted worthy to receive these things at God's hands.

---

[1] In the second century, Christians still greeted one another with a holy kiss. (Rom. 16:16; 1 Pet. 5:14) *See* Tertullian *On Prayer* 18; Athenagoras *Plea for the Christians* 32.

[2] In the early church, the cup always contained wine mixed with water, rather than pure wine. *See* Clement *Instructor* 2. 2; Cyprian *Epistle* 62. Apparently, this represented the blood and water that flowed from Jesus' side at the cross. (John 19:34) Many churches today still follow this custom.

When he is finished praying and giving thanks, all the people who are present express their assent by saying "amen." This word *amen* means in the Hebrew language, "So be it." After the presiding brother has given thanks and all the people have given their assent, the ones called servants [deacons] give to each person who is present the bread and wine mixed with water, over which the thanksgiving was given, so they can partake. They also take a portion to those who are absent.

We call this food "thanksgiving" [Greek: *Eucharistia*].[3] The only ones allowed to partake of this are those who believe that the things we teach are true, who have been washed with the washing that is for the forgiveness of sins and for spiritual rebirth, and who live by the teachings of Christ.[4] For we do not receive these as just ordinary bread and drink. But Jesus Christ our Saviour became human by the word of God—having both flesh and blood for our salvation. So we have been taught that the food which is blessed by the prayer of his word is the flesh and blood of that Jesus who was made flesh.[5] Our blood and flesh are nourished from it by transmutation.

The apostles, in their memoirs, which are called "good news" [gospels], have passed on to us the things Jesus commanded them. They relate that Jesus took bread, and after giving thanks, said, "This is my body. Do this in remembrance of me." And in like manner, having taken the cup and given thanks, he said, "This is my blood," and gave it to them alone. [Luke 22:19]

---

[3] 1 Cor. 10:16.

[4] Titus 3:5; Acts 2:38; 22:16; 1 Cor. 11:27-29.

[5] Justin's statement about the significance of the bread and wine has been a source of controversy among theologians for centuries. Although it has been quoted by Catholics, Lutherans, and Calvinists alike to support their varying interpretations, it seems that Justin understood Jesus' words fairly literally. However, other early Christians, such as Clement of Alexandria, understood Jesus' words figuratively. (Clement *Instructor* 1.6) Although the early Christians had differing opinions about the Eucharist, there are no recorded divisions or theological disputes in the first three centuries over this issue. Perhaps we would all do well to imitate their spirit of tolerance.

As might be expected, the wicked demons have imitated this in the mysteries of Mithras, commanding the same thing to be done. You may already know, or can learn, that in their mystic rites, bread and a cup of water, over which incantations are said, are given to those being initiated.

After these things are done, we continually remind each other of these things. The wealthy among us help the needy. And we stay together. We thank the Maker of all, through his Son Jesus Christ and through the Holy Spirit, for all the things he has given us. On the day called Sunday, all who live in cities or in the country gather together to one place. There the memoirs of the apostles, or the writings of the prophets, are read, for as long as time permits. When the reader is finished, the presiding brother verbally instructs us and urges us to imitate the good things that were read to us. Next we all rise together and pray. And as I related before, when our prayer is ended, bread and wine and water are brought.[6] In like manner, the presiding brother offers prayers and thanksgiving according to his ability. And the people assent, saying, "Amen." Then the bread and wine are distributed to each person, and each partakes. The servants [deacons] take a portion to those who are absent.

Those who are well to do, and are willing, give what they think fit. The funds collected are deposited with the presiding brother, who helps the orphans and widows, together with others in need because of sickness or any other reason. He also assists the prisoners, and any strangers who happen to be among us. In short, he takes care of all who are in need.

Sunday is the day on which we all hold our common meeting, because it is the first day on which God made the world, having worked a change in the darkness and matter.[7] On this same day, Jesus Christ our Savior rose from the dead. He was crucified on the day before that of Saturn.[8] On the day after that of Saturn, which is the day of the sun,[9] he appeared to his apostles and disciples and thereafter taught them many of the things I have submitted to you for your consideration.

---

[6] The early Christians observed communion every Sunday. *See* Cyprian *Epistle* 62.

[7] Acts 20:7.

[8] The "day of Saturn" refers to Saturday.

[9] The "day of the sun" refers to Sunday.

7

We Refuse To Worship Demons And Idols

We refuse to believe godless teachings and we pledge ourselves to do no wickedness. Yet you punish us without restraint instead of examining the charges made against us. You give in to the instigation of evil demons. But I'm going to tell you the truth about demons. Since ancient times, the evil demons have made ghostly appearances to humans, defiling women and corrupting boys. They have made such terrifying appearances to men that those who did not maintain reason [*logos*] were struck with horror. In their fear, not realizing that these beings were demons, men called them gods. They gave to these "gods" whatever names the demons chose for themselves.

We are not the first to say this.† Socrates tried to bring these facts to light, using true reason [*logos*] and careful investigation. He tried to free men from the control of these demons. However, the demons used their human subjects to label him as an atheist, and thereby brought about his death. The demons are now using the same tactics against us.

However, it was not only among the Greeks that reason [*logos*] broke through the wall of superstition with the help of men like Socrates. In fact, among those people you call barbarians, Reason [*Logos*] took on shape and became a man—a man named Jesus Christ. In obedience to Christ, we not only deny that the beings of mythology are really gods, but we declare unequivocally that they are wicked demons. Their actions do not even meet the standards of righteous humans.

We have come from every race of men, and many of us used to worship Bacchus and Apollo (whose lustful exploits are too shameful to mention). We used to worship the love-maddened Proserpina and Venus, whose mysteries you still celebrate. But now through Jesus Christ, we have learned to disdain those gods, even though we are threatened with death as a result. Instead, we dedicate ourselves to the Un-begotten God. And we are convinced that he is not filled with base lusts as are Jupiter and the other "gods." We pity those who believe in such mythical gods, for they were invented by demons.

Because we do not worship demons and mythical gods, you call us atheists. And we confess without shame that indeed we are atheists— at least so far as "gods" of this sort are concerned. But with respect to the most true God, the Father of all righteousness, we are most definitely *not* atheists. He is free from all impurity, and we worship and adore him, and the Son (who came forth from him and taught us these things, and the host of the other good angels

> *Because we do not worship demons, you call us atheists.*

who follow him and are made like him), and the prophetic Spirit. We know them in reason [*logos*] and truth. And we freely share the things we have been taught with all who wish to learn.

The Truth About Idols

Furthermore, we do not honor the idols that men call "gods." [1 Cor. 10:14] We refuse to sacrifice to them or anoint them with garlands of flowers. We realize that these idols are lifeless, without spirit. [Ps. 135:15] They are not even in the form of God. For God doesn't have a human form that we can imitate with idols and statues. These idols are really in the form of those wicked demons who have appeared to mankind in the past. [1 Cor. 10:20] I really don't need to tell you about the shapes and forms into which artisans fashion their materials by carving and cutting, casting and hammering. You already know these things. You also know that they often fashion gods out of ordinary bowls and utensils merely by changing their form and shape. [Isa. 44:15-20]

We consider this not only senseless, but *insulting* to God. For one thing, it insults God, who is indescribable in form and in glory, to attach his name to things that are subject to decay and that require constant upkeep. Secondly, the artisans who fashion these idols are often drunkards who are steeped in every type of vice, as you well know. They even corrupt the very girls who work alongside them. What absurdity to think that such degenerate men fashion and create gods for your worship! How ridiculous that these same men serve as the guardians of the temples where your "gods" are enshrined. Don't you realize that it is wrong to even *think* that humans can be the guardians of gods?

> *We have been taught that he accepts only those who imitate his qualities.*

The True Way To Worship God

We have been taught that God does not need the material offerings men bring. He himself is the Provider of all things. We have been taught, are convinced, and do believe that he accepts only those who imitate his qualities: self-control, justice, love, and those other virtues that are unique to a God who is called by no proper name. We have also been taught that in the beginning, out of his goodness, he created all things out of unformed matter for the sake of man. We have been taught that if men by their works show themselves to be worthy of his design, he deems them deserving to reign in company with him and to be delivered from all corruption and suffering. [Rev. 22:12; 2 Cor. 5:10] So those who choose what is pleasing to him are, because of their choice, considered worthy of incorruption and of fellowship with him. And in order that we may follow the things which please him, he has given us the power of reason [*logos*]. He also persuades us and leads us to faith.

We consider it important to teach these things to all people. In fact, the teachings of the Logos, because he is Divine, would have already touched most of mankind, if it were not for the wicked demons. They have manipulated the seed of wickedness that exists in all mankind and have spread many false accusations against us.

From what I have already said, I think any reasonable person will acknowledge that we are not atheists since we worship the Maker of the universe. We simply have been taught that he has no need for blood sacrifices, offerings, and incense. [Heb. 10:1-4] Yet we do praise him to the utmost of our ability, through our prayers and thanksgiving, for all the things he has supplied us. We have been taught that it does not honor him to burn on the altar the very things he has created for our sustenance. Instead, we gratefully use such things for ourselves and for those who are in need. We offer prayers and hymns of thanksgiving to God for our creation, for our health, for the wonderful changes of seasons, and for everything else he has given us. And we petition him that, after we die, we might be resurrected to an incorruptible life, through faith in him.

The person who taught us all these things is none other than Jesus Christ himself, who was brought into the world for this very purpose. He was crucified under Pontius Pilate, governor of Judea during the days of Tiberius Caesar. It is only reasonable that we worship him, since we have learned that he is the Son of the true God himself. We hold him in the second place and the prophetic Spirit in the third. We realize that you think us insane to give to a crucified man a place second to the unchangeable and eternal God, the Creator of all. But that's because you do not discern the mystery about these things. However, I will make it plain to you, and I only ask that you pay attention to what I am about to tell you.*

---

*The early Christians' understanding of the Trinity differed somewhat from what is generally taught today. Most Christians today think of the Trinity in terms of a horizontal plane:

Father—Son—Holy Spirit

However, the early Christians generally thought of the Trinity in terms of a vertical succession:

Father
|
Son
|
Holy Spirit

Their understanding was based on such passages as "I did not speak of my own accord, but the Father who sent me commanded me what to say and how to say it" (John 12:49); and "When he has done this, then the Son himself will be made subject to him who put everything under him, so that God may be all in all." (1 Cor. 15:28) Justin explains the early Christian view in more detail in his *Conversation with Trypho*. *See also* Tertullian *Against Praxeas*; Irenaeus *Against Heresies* 2.28; Clement of Alexandria *Miscellanies* 7.1,2; Theophilus *Autolycus* 22; Hippolytus *Against Noetus*; and Origen *Against Celsus* 2.9; 8.9-15.

8

How The Demons Mislead Mankind

In case some of you think that we teach that Christ was born only 150 years ago under Cyrenius, that he taught for the first time during the days of Pontius Pilate, and that anyone who was born before Christ is without responsibility, let me explain our teachings. We have been taught that Christ is the Firstborn of God. As I stated before, we also believe that he is the Logos of whom every race of men have been partakers. And so anyone who has lived by reason [*logos*] was really a Christian, even though he was called an atheist. For example, among the Greeks there were such men as Socrates and Heraclitus.* Among the barbarians, there were Abraham, Elijah, Hananiah, Mishael, and Azariah [Shadrach, Meshach, and Abednego], and countless others. Anyone who lived apart from reason [*logos*] and killed those who lived reasonably, actually opposed Christ—even though he lived *before* Christ's human birth.

Through the power of the Logos, according to the will of God, the Father and Lord of all, Christ was born as a human

---

*Most Christians would probably not have been quite as charitable in regarding seekers of truth, such as Socrates, as being "Christians before Christ." Nevertheless, many Christians did see them as honest men who sought after God and, as such, might be saved.

through a virgin. He was named Jesus, was crucified, rose from the dead, and ascended into heaven.

After Christ's ascension into heaven, these demons produced various men who claimed to be gods. Yet you did not persecute these men, but showered them with honor instead. For example, there was Simon, a Samaritan who did mighty acts of magic in the imperial city of Rome during the reign of Claudius Caesar. He did those acts through demonic power; nevertheless, you considered him a god and honored him with a statue erected on the river Tiber between the two bridges. The inscription on his statue reads, "To Simon the holy god."*

In fact, nearly all the Samaritans, and some people from other nations, worship Simon and confess him as their primary god. His worshipers even say that a former prostitute named Helena, who was his close companion, was the First Concept generated by him. If any of you are still entangled in Simon's teachings, we pray you will learn the truth about him and escape his errors. As for his statue, it is my humble recommendation that you destroy it.

There was also a disciple of Simon named Meander, possessed by demons, who deceived many people with his magical arts while he was in Antioch. He convinced his listeners that they would never die. Some people still hold to his teachings.

Finally, there is also a man named Marcion, who is still living. By the aid of demons, he has taught many people of all nations to deny that God is the Maker of the universe. Instead, he says that there is some other Being, greater than God, who has done greater works.

Unfortunately, the disciples of all three of these men are called Christians, the same as we are. Perhaps the disciples of these three men are guilty of the deeds of which you accuse

*Justin is speaking of the same Simon who tried to purchase the gifts of the Spirit from Peter (Acts 8:9-24). He was severely rebuked by Peter, and he initially repented. However, his repentance was obviously short lived, and before long he returned to his old ways. Many other early Christian writers discuss his heresy.

us: promiscuous sex relations and cannibalism. I don't know. But I do know that you neither persecute them nor put them to death on account of their beliefs. If you would like to know more about these groups, I have written a work against all the heresies. I will give it to you if you would like to read it.

The Demons Mislead Through Imitation

The demons' sole purpose seems to be to seduce mankind from God, their Creator, and from Christ, his First-Begotten. [1 Tim. 4:1; 2 Thess. 2:9,10] The demons make sure that those people who cannot raise their thoughts above earthly things stay attached to earthly things and to the works of their own hands. They also secretly attack those who devote their lives to contemplation of divine things. Unless such persons are wise and sober-minded, and unless they live with purity, free from lust, the demons lure them into godlessness.

One way the demons mislead mankind is by imitating the things of the true God.[†] For example, they have imitated the writings of Moses by teaching that Proserpina was the daughter of Jupiter, and they have instigated the people to set up an image of her under the name of Cora at the spring heads of the waters. For Moses had written, "In the beginning God made the heaven and the earth. And the earth was without form and unfurnished. And the Spirit of God moved upon the face of the waters" [Gen. 1:1,2]. In imitation of the Spirit of God moving on the waters, they said that Proserpina was the daughter of Jupiter.

Similarly, the demons taught that Minerva was the daughter of Jupiter, but not by sexual union. Instead, knowing that God conceived and made the world by his Logos, they say that Minerva is the First Concept. We consider it to be quite absurd that they bring forward the Concept of God in a female shape. And likewise, the deeds of those others who are called sons of Jupiter are sufficient to condemn them.

The demons, having heard the prophet Isaiah speak of the washing of rebirth, decided to institute their own imitation ceremony. [Isa. 1:16] So those who enter their temples with food and drink offerings are told to sprinkle themselves. And, after making their sacrifice, they are commanded to wash themselves entirely before entering the shrines where the demons' images are kept.

The practice of removing shoes before entering certain temples is another imitation of God's practices.† When Moses was tending the flocks of his maternal uncle in the land of Arabia, he was ordered to go down into Egypt and lead the Israelite people out from there. Our Christ, appearing to him in the form of fire in a bush, conversed with him and said, "Take off your shoes and come near to hear" [Ex. 3:5]. After Moses had taken off his shoes and walked closer, he was told to go down into Egypt and lead the Israelite people out of there. He also received mighty power from Christ, who spoke to him in the appearance of fire. He went down and led the people out, after having performed great and marvelous works. (If you would like to learn more about these things, you can learn them accurately from the writings of Moses.) And the demons imitate these things by directing their priests to command the worshipers to take off their shoes when entering their temples to worship.

The Demons Did Not Imitate The Cross

However, the demons did not represent any of those mythical gods and sons of Jupiter as being crucified. The reason is that they did not understand the prophecies about Christ's crucifixion, since these prophecies were presented symbolically. Yet, as was foretold by the prophets, the cross is now the greatest symbol of God's power and rule. In fact, we can all observe that the form of the cross is essential to our routine affairs of life.

For example, you make use of the cross every time you sail across the sea, for the mast and crossbeam form a cross. The farmer's plow is of this same shape, as are most of the implements used by mechanics and laborers. Moreover, look at the very shape of the human body and how it differs from that of the irrational animals. We differ from the animals in the fact that we stand erect. And when our arms are extended, we form the shape of the cross. Finally, look at your own banners and military standards. These are also in the shape of a cross.

9

The Jews Do Not Understand The Logos

The Jews still teach that the nameless God spoke directly to Moses. But the Spirit of prophecy accuses them through the prophet Isaiah, "The ox knows his owner; the donkey, his master's crib. But Israel does not know me, and my people do not understand" [Isa. 1:3]. Because the Jews knew neither the Father nor his Son, Jesus Christ accused them, saying, "No one knows the Father but the Son. No one knows the Son but the Father, and those to whom the Son revealed him" [Matt. 11:27].

Now, the Logos of God is God's Son, as I have said before. He is also called "Angel" and "Apostle." The Logos tells us whatever we need to know, and he is sent forth to declare whatever is revealed. As our Lord himself said, "He that hears me, hears him that sent me" [Luke 10:16]. This is also clear from the writings of Moses, which say, "The angel of God spoke to Moses in a flame of fire out of the bush, saying, 'I am that I am, the God of Abraham, the God of Isaac, the God of Jacob, and the God of your fathers. Go down into Egypt and deliver my people'" [Ex. 3:6]. Space does not permit me to relate all the events here, but you can read them in the writings of Moses if you wish to learn what happened after that.

In fact, much is written to prove that Jesus Christ is the Son of God and the Apostle of God. He is the Logos of ancient times. He sometimes appeared in the form of fire; other times, he appeared as an angel. Now, however, by the will of God, he has become man, enduring all of the things that the demons instigated the senseless Jews to inflict on him. They have the writings of Moses, which expressly state: "The *angel* of God spoke to Moses in a flame of fire in a bush and said, 'I am that I am, the God of Abraham, the God of Isaac, and the God of Jacob.'" Yet they maintain that the one who said this was the Father and Creator of the universe. No wonder the Spirit of prophecy rebukes them, saying, "Israel does not know me; my people have not understood me" [Isa. 1:3].

As I have mentioned, Jesus, while he was among them, said, "No one knows the Father but the Son. No one knows the Son but the Father, and those to whom the Son revealed him" [Matt. 11:27].

So the Jews think that it was the Father of the universe who spoke to Moses. But the one who spoke to Moses was actually the Son of God, who is called both Angel and Apostle. And so the Jews are justly charged by both the Spirit of prophecy and by Christ himself with knowing neither the Father nor the Son. Those who think the Son is the Father are shown never to have really been acquainted with the Father. Nor do they know that the Father of the universe has a Son, who—since he is the First-Begotten Logos of God—is true Deity.

> *But the one who spoke to Moses was actually the Son of God.*

In ancient times, Christ appeared to Moses and to the other prophets in the form of fire and in the likeness of an angel. But now in the days of your empire, Christ became man through a virgin, according to the will of the Father, for the salvation of those who believe in him. He became humble and suffered, so that by dying and rising again he could conquer death. The words spoken out of the bush to Moses, "I am that I am, the God of Abraham, and the God of Isaac, and the God of Jacob, and the God of your fathers," signified that those men, even though they are dead, are still in existence and belong to Christ. [Matt. 22:31,32] For they were [among] the first of all men to concern themselves with seeking God. Abraham was the father of Isaac, and Isaac was the father of Jacob, as Moses wrote.

10

The Philosophers Taught Many Of The Same Things We Do

Actually, our teachings should not seem that strange to you.† The philosophers you so admire taught many of the same things we do.† For example, Plato taught that Minos would punish the wicked. That's essentially the same thing we teach, except we say it's Christ who will judge. And we say the wicked will be punished in the *same* bodies they have now, after their bodies and spirits are re-united. Also, we say that their punishment will be everlasting, not merely for a thousand years, as Plato taught.

Again, your prophetesses, called the sibyls, have said that the material universe will be dissolved. The Stoic philosophers teach that even God himself will be consumed by fire in the end, and that the world will be formed anew. However, we believe that God, the Creator of all things, is superior to the things created and will not be transformed with them. So as you can see, on some points we teach no differently than the poets and philosophers you honor. On other points, our teachings are more complete and more divine. And we alone give proof of what we teach. So why do people unjustly hate us?

When we say that God created all things and arranged the universe, we are teaching similarly to Plato. When we say that the world will be consumed by fire, we are saying the same thing as the Stoics. When we declare that souls have sensation after death and that the souls of the wicked will be punished, we are teaching similarly to your poets and philosophers. The same is true when we say that the good will be delivered from punishment and will enjoy a blessed existence. Even when we say that men should not worship the works of their hands, did not the poet Menander and others say the same thing? Didn't they say that the workman is greater than the work he creates?

The Birth, Life, And Death Of Jesus

What about when we say that the Logos, who is the Firstborn of God, was produced without sexual union, and that he, Jesus Christ, our teacher, was crucified, died, rose again, and ascended into heaven? We are saying nothing differently than what you believe about the sons of Jupiter: You believe that Mercury is the interpreting logos and teacher of all. You believe that Aesculapius, the great physician, was struck by a thunderbolt and then ascended to heaven. You teach that Bacchus also ascended to heaven after being torn limb from limb. You say the same about Hercules after he threw himself into the flames. You teach that Perseus and other mortals rose to heaven on the horse Pegasus. Others, you say, were placed among the stars. You deify some of your emperors and even produce witnesses who will say they saw the dead Caesar rise from his funeral pyre and ascend to heaven.

Young students learn about Jupiter and his sons in school. This is supposedly for their edification; for everyone considers it worthwhile to imitate the gods. But think for a minute about these beings you worship as gods. You teach that Jupiter murdered his own parents, yet you say he is the creator and governor of all things. You also say that he was filled with lustful desires and that he and his sons raped many women. That is why we say that it was really wicked demons who perpetrated these things. But we have been taught that only those who live close to God in holiness can be deified. [2 Pet. 1:4] Those who live wickedly and are unrepentant are punished in everlasting fire.

Even if Jesus had been only an ordinary human, born through normal reproduction, he would still deserve to be called the Son of God because of his wisdom. For your writers all call God the father of men and gods. And when we declare that the Logos of God was born of God in a special manner, different from ordinary reproduction, this should not sound so unusual to you who teach that Mercury is the messenger and logos of God.

Some object that Jesus could not be the Son of God because he suffered crucifixion. Yet as I described above, you believe that the sons of Jupiter also suffered and died in various ways. But the deeds of Jesus show him to be superior to those gods.

As for the fact that we teach that Jesus was born of a virgin, you say the same thing about Perseus. When we say that Jesus healed the lame and the blind, is this that much different from what you believe about Aesculapius?

Creation Of The World

Plato taught that God created the world by altering preexistent, shapeless matter. But he borrowed his teaching from our teachers—that is, the prophets. Moses was the first prophet and of greater antiquity than the Greek writers. This is what the Spirit of prophecy told him about the materials from which God formed the world and how God used those materials: "In the beginning God created the heaven and the earth. And the earth was invisible and unfurnished, and darkness was upon the face of the deep. And the Spirit of God moved over the waters. And God said, 'Let there be light'; and it was so" [Gen. 1:1-3].

> *Moses was of greater antiquity than the Greek writers.*

We have learned that by the word of God the whole world was made out of the substance Moses mentioned. Plato and others who agreed with him realized this, too. We are mentioning this so you can be convinced also. In fact, Moses had already spoken of the substance that the poets call "Erebus."

The Logos Of God

Plato spoke about the Son of God in his work entitled *Timaeus*. In that work, he said, "God placed him [the Logos] like an X in the universe." Again, Plato borrowed his thoughts from Moses. In his writings, Moses related how the Israelites, when they were in the wilderness, were attacked by poisonous snakes, both vipers and asps, which killed many people. Under the inspiration and influence of God, Moses took some brass and shaped it into the figure of a cross. He set it in the holy tabernacle and told the people, "If you look at this figure and believe, you will be saved" [Num. 21:8,9]. It is recorded that when this was done, the serpents died and the people were delivered from death.

When he read these things, Plato did not accurately understand that Moses was referring to a figure of a cross, so he said that the Power next to the first God was placed crosswise in the universe. And Plato spoke of a third power because he had read the words of Moses that "the Spirit of God moved over the waters" [Gen. 1:2]. So Plato gives the second place to the Logos who is with God, the one he said was placed crosswise in the universe. And he gives the third place to the Spirit who was said to be borne upon the waters, saying "And the third [Power] was around the third."

Notice how the Spirit of prophecy also revealed through Moses that the world would burn up. He said, "Everlasting fire shall descend and shall devour to the pit beneath" [Deut. 32:22].

We Are Not Copying The Philosophers

Please understand that it is not that we hold the same opinions as these philosophers, but that these, and so many others, speak in imitation of us. In fact, among our people, you can learn these things from persons who are uneducated and unrefined in speech—in fact, from persons who do not even know the letters of the alphabet. Some of them are even physically blind. Yet they are wise and they have believing minds. This is the case so that you can realize that these things have not been produced by human wisdom, but by the power of God.

Please do not misunderstand our position. We do not want you to accept our message simply because we say many of the same things these other writers have said. We want you to accept our message only because what we say is *true*. We preach whatever Christ and the prophets who preceded him taught. These truths are older than all of the Greek and Roman writers. In fact, they alone are true.

You should also know that Jesus Christ is the only actual Son begotten by God. He is the Logos, the First-Begotten, and the Power of God. He became man according to God's will, and he taught us all these things for the conversion and restoration of the human race.

Thirdly, before Christ became a human, some poets—through the inspiration of the demons—wrote myths about the gods. In their myths, the poets portrayed the gods as doing the same things that Christ would do once he appeared on earth.

So Why Do You Hate Only Christians?

Although what we teach is similar in many ways to what the Greeks taught, you hate us. But you do not hate them. So you must hate us because of the name of Christ. Although we do no wrong, you put us to death as though we do wrong.

In some lands, people worship trees and rivers. Others worship mice, cats, or crocodiles. Different animals are worshiped in different countries. In some places, it is one animal; in another place, it is a different animal. So the same animal is viewed as a god by some people, but as simply a wild beast by others. So why should we be condemned simply because we do not worship the same gods you do? Or make offerings for the dead, or crown idols with garlands?

11

Evidence That Jesus Was The Son Of God

Someone might ask, "Isn't it possible that Christ was simply a human who performed mighty works through the magical arts and thereby only *appeared* to be the Son of God?" However, our belief in Christ as the Son of God is not based merely on the assertion of others; it is founded on compelling evidence. What originally convinced me and many others is the fact that the events surrounding the life of Jesus were foretold in advance. We have witnessed with our very eyes that things have happened just as they were predicted. When you read these prophesies, we think you will also acknowledge that these are the strongest and truest evidence.

The Jewish Prophecies

Centuries ago, there were certain men among the Jews who were prophets of God. Through these men, the prophetic Spirit foretold things that would happen in the future. As these prophecies were spoken, the prophets arranged them in books in their own Hebrew language, and the various kings of the Jews preserved them. When Ptolemy, King of Egypt, formed a library, he attempted to collect together the writings of all mankind. When he heard of these

Jewish prophets, he requested Herod, who was king of the Jews at that time, to send him copies of the books of the prophets. Herod sent copies to him, but they were in the Hebrew language. As a result, the Egyptians could not understand the writings. So Ptolemy sent his messengers back to Herod and asked him to commission translators to come and translate the Jewish writings into the Greek language. This was done, and the books remained with the Egyptians, where they still can be found to this day.*

These writings are also in the possession of Jews throughout the world. However, although the Jews can read these things, they do not understand them. As a result, they treat us as enemies. And as you can imagine, they abuse us and even kill us whenever they are in a position to do so—the same way you do. In the recent Jewish wars, Bar-Cochba, the leader of the Jewish revolt, gave orders that the Christians— and only the Christians—should be tortured unless they would deny Jesus Christ and blaspheme God.

In the books of the prophets, we find prophecies about Jesus our Christ. They foretold his coming. His being born of a virgin and growing as a man. His healing every type of disease and sickness and even raising the dead. His being unrecognized and hated. His crucifixion, death, and resurrection. His ascension into heaven. And his being the Son of God. It was also predicted that he would send persons into every nation to proclaim these things and that it would be primarily the Gentiles who would believe in him. His appearance was predicted by a succession of prophets through the centuries. The first was 5000 years in advance. Others were 3000 years in advance. Then 2000 years. Then 1000 years. And finally 800 years in advance.

Prophecies Of Moses

Moses, the first of these prophets, foretold the coming of Christ when he prophesied: "The scepter shall not depart from Judah, nor a lawgiver from between his feet, until he

---

* Justin is speaking about the Greek Septuagint version. Ptolemy actually made his request to Eleazor the high priest (c. 250 B.C.), not to Herod.

comes for whom it is reserved. And he shall be the desire of the nations, binding his foal to the vine, washing his robe in the blood of the grapes" [Gen. 49:10]. You can inquire and determine for yourselves that the Jews had a lawgiver and king of their own until the time of Jesus Christ, our teacher. He interpreted various prophecies that were not yet understood. This was just as the holy and divine Spirit of prophecy had foretold through Moses, saying that a ruler would not fail the Jews until he should come for whom the kingdom was reserved. (The name "Jews" comes from Judah, their forefather). After Christ appeared, you Romans began to rule the Jews and gained possession of their territories. In fact, after Jesus was crucified, the land of the Jews was surrendered to you as a spoil of war.*

The prophetic words, "he shall be the expectation of the nations," signified that there would be people in all nations who would look for him to return. Again, this is something you can plainly verify for yourself. For among all peoples, there are some who are eagerly awaiting the return of him who was crucified. The prophecy "binding his foal to the vine, and washing his robe in the blood of the grape" symbolized the things that were to happen to Christ and what Christ would do. For shortly before his death, a foal of a donkey stood tied to a vine at the entrance of a village. Jesus told his companions to bring it to him. After it was brought to him, he mounted it and rode it into Jerusalem, where the vast temple of the Jews stood. [Luke 19:28-37] You later destroyed this temple. After this he was crucified, which fulfilled the rest of the prophecy. The "washing his robe in the blood of the grape" referred to the suffering he was to endure, cleansing by his blood all those who believe in him.

What the divine Spirit calls "his robe" are those people who believe in him and in whom abides the seed of God, the Logos. "The blood of the grapes" signifies that the Christ would have blood, like other humans, but that his blood was

* Rome began its rule over Palestine in 63 B.C., but the Jews had their own nominal ruler up until a few decades before Jesus was born. In 70 A.D., a few decades after Jesus' death, the Romans captured and despoiled Jerusalem, destroying its temple.

not produced through the seed of man, but by the power of God. The first Power after God, the Father and Lord of all, is the Logos, who is also the Son.

The Virgin Birth Of Christ

Now I will tell you how he took flesh and became man. Since the blood of the vine is produced by God, not by man, it signified that his blood would not be produced by human seed but by the power of God.

Isaiah, another prophet, prophesied the same things in other words, saying, "A star shall rise out of Jacob, and a flower shall spring from the root of Jesse. The nations shall trust his arm" [Isa. 11:1]. In fact, a star of light *has* risen. A flower *has* sprung forth from the root of Jesse. It is Christ himself. For by the power of God, he was conceived by a virgin of the line of Jacob. Jacob, in turn, was the father of Judah, who as I have already said was the forefather of the Jews. The prophecy said that Jesse would be a forefather of Jesus, and he was. He was a lineal descendant of both Jacob and Judah.

Isaiah also foretold that Christ would be born of a virgin, saying, "Look! A virgin shall conceive and bring forth a son. And they shall call his name, 'God with us'" [Isa. 7:14]. God predicted these things through the Spirit of prophecy even though they seemed impossible to men. God did this so that once the prophecies came to pass, there would be faith rather than unbelief. Please do not think that we are saying the same things as the poets who say that Jupiter had lustful relations with women. When the prophecy says, "Look! A virgin shall conceive," it means that she would conceive without sexual relations. If she had had sexual relations with anyone—even if it had been with God—she would no longer have been a virgin. Instead, the power of God came upon the virgin, overshadowing her. It caused her to conceive while she was still a virgin. [Luke 1:34,35] An angel sent by God brought this good news to the virgin, saying, "Look! You will conceive by the Holy Spirit and shall bear a son. And he shall be called son of the highest. And you shall call his name Jesus, for he shall save his people from their sins" [Luke 1:32].

The men who have recorded all the things concerning our Savior Jesus are the ones who have taught us these things. Since Isaiah had also prophesied about these things, we have believed them. It is wrong, therefore, to understand the Spirit and the Power of God to be anything other than the Logos, who is also the Firstborn of God, as the prophet Moses had declared. [1 Cor. 1:24] This is what caused the virgin to conceive when it overshadowed her. The conception did not come by sexual relations, but by power.

The name "Jesus" in the Hebrew language means the same thing as "Savior" in the Greek language. That is why the angel said to the virgin, "You shall call his name Jesus, for he shall save his people from their sins." Even you will acknowledge that all true prophets are inspired by none other than the divine Logos.

12

Other Prophecies About Jesus

Almost every facet of Jesus' life—from the place of his birth to the manner of his death—were foretold by the Jewish prophets.[†]

The Place Of Jesus' Birth

The prophet Micah foretold the place of his birth, saying: "And you, Bethlehem, the land of Judah, are not the least among the princes of Judah. For out of you will come a ruler who will feed my people" [Mic. 5:2]. Jesus Christ was born in Bethlehem, a village in the land of the Jews, thirty-five stadia [about four miles] from Jerusalem.

The Life And Crucifixion Of Jesus

It was also prophesied that after Christ was born he was to live unnoticed until he reached manhood. This happened just as predicted. There was also the following prediction: "Unto us a child is born, and unto us a young man is given, and the government shall be upon his shoulders" [Isa. 9:6]. This predicted the power of the cross, for he applied his shoulders to it when he was crucified.

This same prophet, Isaiah, was inspired by the prophetic Spirit to say, "I have spread out my hands to a disobedient and obstinate people, to those who walk in a way that is not good. They now ask judgment of me and dare to draw near to God" [Isa. 65:2]. Through David, who was both a king and a prophet, the Spirit foretold: "They pierced my hands and feet. They cast lots for my clothing" [Ps. 22:16]. David did not experience any of those things. Instead, it was Jesus Christ

> *We who used to murder one another no longer make war on our enemies.*

who stretched forth his hands, being crucified by the Jews who spoke against him and who denied that he was the Christ. Just as the prophet had foretold, they sneered at him and set him upon the judgment seat and said, "Judge us." The expression, "They pierced my hands and feet," refers to the nails of the cross that were hammered into his hands and feet. After he was crucified, the soldiers cast lots for his clothing, and they divided his clothes among themselves. You can verify from the official records of Pontius Pilate that all of these things happened.

Christ's Entry Into Jerusalem

I will also cite the prophecy of another prophet named Zephaniah, who specifically foretold that Christ would enter Jerusalem riding the foal of a donkey: "Rejoice, oh daughter of Zion! Shout, oh daughter of Jerusalem! Behold, your king comes to you, lowly, and riding upon a donkey, upon a colt, the foal of a donkey" [Zech. 9:9].

The Disciples Of Jesus

The Spirit of prophecy also foretold what the apostles of Jesus would do.[†] "For out of Zion shall go forth the law, and the word of the Lord from Jerusalem. And he shall judge among the nations and shall rebuke many people. And they shall beat their swords into plowshares and their spears into pruning hooks. Nation shall not lift up sword against nation, neither shall they learn war any more" [Isa. 2:3,4]. And this came to pass, as I will explain. Out of Jerusalem went twelve men. They were illiterate and unpolished in speech. [Acts 4:13] But by the power of God they proclaimed to every people group that they had been sent by Christ to teach the word of God to the whole world. [Matt. 28:16-20] And we who used to murder one another no longer make war on our enemies. [2 Cor. 10:3,4]

Not only that, we prefer to confess Christ and die, than to lie and deceive our accusers. Of course, we could follow your precept, "The tongue has sworn, but the mind remains unsworn." Yet, the soldiers enrolled by you, who are bound by a military oath, prefer to die than to break their oath of allegiance. In fact, they are willing to give up parents, their place of living, and all their relatives rather than to break their oath. Nevertheless, you cannot offer them anything that is imperishable. That being the case, isn't it only reasonable that we are willing to endure all things in order to obtain our promised reward of imperishable things from the One who is able to grant it?

King David, through the Spirit of prophecy, also prophesied about the men who would proclaim the coming of Christ and who would explain his teachings: "Day unto day utters speech, and night unto night shows knowledge. There is no speech nor language where their voice is not heard. Their voice has gone out into all the earth, and their words to the ends of the world" [Ps. 19:2-6].

The prophet David also foretold that God, the Father of all, would bring Christ to heaven after he had raised him from the dead. He foretold that God would keep Christ in heaven until he had subdued His enemies, the demons. He has delayed the consummation of all things until the number of those who are foreknown by him to be good and virtuous is complete. [1 Pet. 1:2; 2 Pet. 3:9] David prophesied, "The Lord said unto my Lord, sit at my

> *You can do no more than to kill us, and that does us no real harm.*

right hand until I make your enemies your footstool. The Lord will send you the rod of power from Jerusalem. Rule in the midst of your enemies! With you is the government in the day of your power, in the beauty of your saints. Before the morning star, I have begotten you" [Ps. 110:1-3].

When he said, "He will send you the rod of power out of Jerusalem," David predicted the mighty word of Jesus that his apostles, going forth from Jerusalem, preached everywhere. Even though death is decreed against those who teach about Jesus, or even confess the name of Christ, we still embrace his name and teach about him everywhere. If what I have said angers you, you can do no more than to kill us, as I said before. And that does us no real harm. But it brings eternal punishment by fire to you and to all who unjustly hate us, unless you repent. [Matt. 10:28]

The Devastation Of Jerusalem

The Spirit of prophecy also foretold that the land of the Jews would be devastated. For example, the following words were spoken as though they came from the mouths of the Jewish people who wondered about what had happened: "Zion is a wilderness; Jerusalem, a desolation. The house of our sanctuary has become a curse, and the glory which our fathers blessed is burned up with fire. All its glorious things are laid waste. You have refrained yourself at these things and have held your peace. You have sorely humbled us" [Isa. 64:10-12].

You, of course, know that Jerusalem has been devastated, just as it was predicted. Isaiah prophesied about its desolation and the fact that no one would be permitted to inhabit it: "Their land is desolate. Their enemies consume it before them, and none of them shall dwell in it" [Isa. 1:7]. You are well aware that it is guarded by you so that no one may dwell in it. You have decreed death for any Jew caught entering it.

The Healing Miracles Of Jesus

It was also foretold that our Christ would heal all types of diseases and raise the dead, as follows: "At his coming, the lame shall leap as the hart, and the tongue of the stammerer shall be clear speaking. The blind shall see, and the lepers shall be cleansed. And the dead shall rise and walk about" [Isa. 35:6]. You can verify from the official records of Pontius Pilate that Christ did those very things.

The Conversion Of The Gentiles

The same Isaiah foretold that the Gentile nations who were not looking for Christ would worship him, but that the Jews who were looking for the Christ would not recognize him when he came. In this instance, the words are spoken as though they came from the person of Christ himself: "I was revealed to those who did not ask for me. I was found by those not seeking me. I said, 'Here I am' to a nation that did not call upon my name" [Isa. 65:1-3]. Although the Jews had the prophecies and were waiting for the coming of Christ, they failed to recognize him when he came. Not only that, they even abused him. In contrast, the Gentiles, who had never even heard about Christ, were filled with joy and faith when they heard the testimony of the apostles who came from Jerusalem and when they heard these prophecies. They turned away from their idols and dedicated themselves to the Unbegotten God through Christ.

The Spirit of prophecy calls the Jewish and Samaritan races the "tribes of Israel" and the "house of Jacob." He calls all the other races "Gentiles." Notice how it was prophesied that more of the Gentiles would be believers than those of the Jews and Samaritans: "Rejoice, barren woman, you without children! Break forth and shout, you who had no birth pangs! For the children of the barren one are more than those of her who had a husband" [Isa. 54:1]. At that time, all the Gentiles were barren of the true God, serving the works of their hands. However, even though the Jews and Samaritans had the word of God from the prophets and were waiting for the coming of Christ, only a few of them recognized him when he came. Speaking in the person of those few, the prophet said, "If the Lord had not left us a seed, we would have been as Sodom and Gomorrah" [Isa.1:9]. Moses tells us that Sodom and Gomorrah were cities of ungodly people that God overthrew, burning them with fire and sulphur. None of their inhabitants were spared, other than a stranger among them named Lot—a Chaldean by birth. He and his daughters were rescued. Anyone who wishes to can visit the site of those cities. The site is still desolate, burned over, and barren.

Finally, I will quote from another prophecy of Isaiah to show it was foretold that more Gentiles would be believers and that they would be truer than the Jews. Isaiah said, "The Gentiles are uncircumcised in the *flesh*, but Israel is uncircumcised in *heart*" [Jer. 9:26].

I could quote many other prophecies, but I feel that these are sufficient to convince those who have ears to hear and understand. I think it is obvious that we are not like those who tell fables about the so-called sons of Jupiter. They talk, but they have no proof of what they say. Why do you think we believe that a crucified man is the Firstborn of the Unbegotten God? Why do we believe that this same man will judge the whole world? We believe because of the prophecies spoken about him before he came into the world and was made man. We see that things have happened just as they were foretold. We have seen the devastation of the land of the Jews, just as it had been foretold. We see people of every nation who have been convinced by the teachings of the apostles and have turned away from the old traditions by which they had previously lived. As one of them myself, I see that the Gentile Christians are both more numerous and more faithful than those from among the Jews and Samaritans.

I feel that these prophecies I have quoted are sufficient to convince anyone who is open-minded, free of prejudices, and truth-seeking.

Future Prophecies

I have shown that everything has happened exactly the way the prophets predicted it would. Shouldn't this convince us that their prophecies about things that are still in the future will happen just as they predicted? Take note that the prophets predicted two different comings of Christ. First he would come as a dishonored and suffering man. This has already occurred. Then he would come from heaven with glory, accompanied by his host of angels. At that time he will raise the bodies of everyone. [Matt. 25:31,32] He will clothe the bodies of the worthy with immortality. He will send the bodies of the wicked, endowed with eternal sensibility, into everlasting fire with the wicked demons.

The prophet Ezekiel said concerning the resurrection of the dead: "Joint shall be joined to joint, bone to bone, and flesh will grow again. Every knee will bow to the Lord and every tongue shall confess him" [Ezek. 37:7,8; Phil. 2:10].

Hear what the prophet said about the punishment and sensation of the wicked: "Their worm will not rest, and their fire shall not be quenched" [Isa. 66:24]. Although the wicked may repent once that happens, it will be to no avail.

The prophet Zechariah foretold what the Jews will do and say when they see him coming in glory: "I will command the four winds to gather the scattered children. I will command the north wind to bring them, and the south wind, that it might not hold back. And then in Jerusalem there will be great lamentation—not the lamentation of mouths or of lips, but the lamentation of the heart. They will rend their hearts, rather than their garments. They will mourn tribe by tribe and then they will look on him whom they have pierced. And they will say, 'Why, oh Lord have you made us err from your way? The glory that our fathers blessed has been turned into shame for us'" [Zech. 12:3-14; Isa 63:17; 64:11].

13

What We Believe About Predestination

Because of those prophecies, you might suppose that we teach that all things happen by fate. But that isn't so. We have learned from the prophets (and we believe it to be true) that punishments and rewards are rendered according to the merit of each man's actions. [Rom. 2:6,7] If this were not the case, and all things happened by fate instead, then nothing would be in our own power. If it were predestined that one person be good and another be wicked, then the first person would not deserve praise nor would the second be worthy of blame. In short, unless humans have the power to choose good and avoid evil, they are not accountable for their actions.

However, I will demonstrate that humans, by their own free choice, may either live uprightly or stumble in sin. For example, we observe that some persons change their course of life. If it had been predestined that those persons would be either good or bad, how would they be capable of doing both good and evil? How can they change from one extreme to the other? Does fate act in opposition to itself? Actually, if predestination were true, we could not say that some people are good and others are bad. Rather, unavoidable destiny would be the cause of evil, not man. In the end, we would have to say that there is neither good nor evil, but that things are only considered such by opinion. But that is the greatest impiety and wickedness, as truth shows.

I will concede that one thing *has* been predestined: those who choose good will receive worthy rewards, and those who choose the opposite will receive worthy punishment. God did not create man in the same way he made the trees and the unreasoning animals. A person would not be worthy of reward or praise if he did not choose to do good on his own, but were merely created for that purpose. Likewise, an evil person would not

> **Unless humans have the power to choose good and avoid evil, they are not accountable for their actions.**

deserve punishment, because he would not be evil of his own doing. He simply could do nothing other than what he was made for.

Man Was Given Free Will

The Holy Spirit of prophecy has taught us that man has the freedom of choice. Through Moses he told us that God said to the first man, "Look! Before your face are both good and evil. Choose the good" [Gen. 2:16,17; Deut. 30:15,19]. And again, God the Father said through the prophet Isaiah: "Wash and be clean! Put away all evil from your souls. Learn to practice righteousness. Care for the orphan and plead for the widow. Come, let us reason together, says the Lord. Although your sins may be scarlet, I will make them white as wool. Even though they may be crimson red I will make them white as snow. And if you are willing and obey me, you will eat the good of the land. But if you do not obey me, the sword will devour you. For the mouth of the Lord has spoken it" [Isa. 1:16-20].

You should note that the expression, "the sword will devour you," does not mean that the disobedient shall be slain by the sword. Rather, the sword of God is fire. Those who choose to live wickedly will be the fuel for God's fire. That is why the prophet added, "for the mouth of the Lord has spoken it." If he were referring to a literal sword that cuts and immediately kills, he would not have used the word "devour."

Plato himself taught similarly, saying, "The blame is on the one who chooses. God himself is blameless." Actually, Plato took this teaching from the prophet Moses, for Moses is more ancient than all the Greek writers. In fact, as I've said before, all the things that the philosophers and poets have taught about the immortality of the soul and punishments after death have come from the writings of the prophets. So have their sayings about heavenly things. It was the writings of the prophets that enabled the Greek poets and philosophers to understand such things. In fact, there seem to be seeds of truth scattered among all peoples. [Rom. 1:21] But often their teachers do not accurately understand the truth, and they end up teaching contradictory things.

> *There seem to be seeds of truth scattered among all peoples.*

When we say that future events are foretold, we do not mean that they happen by fatal necessity. Rather, we mean that God knows in advance everything that everyone will do. [Isa. 46:9,10] And he decreed in advance that these future actions will be rewarded according to their merits. So he foretold through the Spirit of prophecy that he would bestow just rewards according to the merits of each man's actions. He constantly urges humans to repent, demonstrating that he cares and provides for mankind. [2 Pet. 3:9; Acts 17:30]

But by the instigation of the demons, governments have decreed that those who read the books of Hystaspes, or the sibyls, or the Jewish prophets will be put to death. The demons wish to keep men from receiving the knowledge of the good by reading those works. Instead, they want to retain mankind in slavery to themselves. Fortunately, they have not always succeeded; we not only fearlessly read them, but we bring them in the open for your inspection, knowing that their contents will be pleasing to everyone. Even if we persuade only a few, our reward will be very great. As good stewards, we will receive the reward from the Master.

14

Conclusion

In conclusion, if these things seem to you to be reasonable and true, honor them. If they seem nonsensical to you, then treat them as nonsense. But if that's the case, do not decree death against those who have done no wrong, as though they were your enemies. We warn you that you will not escape the coming judgment of God if you continue on your path of injustice. Instead, we invite you to do what is pleasing to God.

You should be aware that we could demand just treatment based on the letter of your father, the great and illustrious Emperor Hadrian. A copy of his letter on behalf of the Christians is attached to this plea. However, we do not petition you primarily on the basis of Emperor Hadrian's decision. Rather, we humbly entreat you with this written explanation simply on the basis that what we ask is just.

The Letter Of Hadrian On Behalf Of The Christians

[addressed to Minucius Fundanus]

I have received the letter addressed to me by your predecessor, Serenius Granianus, a most illustrious man. But I cannot remain silent concerning this matter, lest innocent persons be harmed and informers be encouraged to practice villainy. Therefore, if the inhabitants of your province are willing to back up this petition of theirs by bringing formal accusations against the Christians in a court of law, I do not prohibit them from so doing. But I will not permit them to make use of mere entreaties and outcries. If someone chooses to bring a formal accusation, it is far more just for a court of law to pass judgment. Accordingly, if anyone brings an accusation against the Christians and furnishes proof that these people are doing something contrary to our laws, then you should punish them as their offenses deserve. But give special heed to this, by Hercules, that if any person maliciously brings a false accusation against any of these people, you shall punish him more severely, in proportion to his wickedness!

Biographical Glossary

Aesculapius (ESS kyoo LAY pee us) Roman god of medicine and healing.

Apollo (uh PAUL oh) Greek and Roman god of music, poetry, prophecy, and the sun.

Astarte (as TAR tee) Phonecian goddess of the moon, fertility, and sexual love.

Bacchus (BACK us) Greek and Roman god of wine and revelry.

Bar-Cochba (bar COKE vah) Leader of a widespread Jewish rebellion against the Romans from 132-135 A.D. The revolt was initially successful, but was eventually put down by the Romans.

Bel (bale) Babylonian god of heaven and earth.

Caecilius (sigh SILL ee us) One of the three characters in *Octavius*. Although the work never specifically identifies his relationship to Mark Felix, he apparently was either a trusted employee or a relative of Mark Felix.

Caesar, Claudius (CLAW dee us SEE zerr) A stepgrandson of Augustus. He succeeded Caligula as Emperor of Rome, and reigned from 41-54 A.D.

Caesar, Julius (JOOL ee us SEE zerr) *100-44 B.C.* Skilled Roman general and statesman, who headed successful campaigns in Gaul and Britain. He defeated the forces of Pompey, a rival Roman general, and became benign dictator of the Roman Empire. He was murdered by a group of Roman nobles.

Camillus (kah MILL us) Roman military leader and ruler who saved Rome from invasion by the Gauls. He died about 367 B.C.

Cora (CORE uh) Another name for Proserpina, the wife of Pluto.

Cyrenius (si REE neh us) Roman governor of Syria at the time of Jesus' birth.

Diana (dye ANN uh) Roman goddess of the moon, hunting, and virginity.

Dionysius the Younger (DYE eh NISH ee us) Unpopular despotic Greek tyrant who ruled from 367 to 356 B.C. and again from 347-344 B.C. He was eventually overthrown by his subjects.

Epicureans (EP ih kyoo REE ens) The followers of the Greek philosopher Epicurus (c. 342-270 B.C.). They believed that the goal of life should be the obtainment of pleasure. However, they considered temperance, serenity, and cultural development to be the foremost pleasures. They also believed in the atomic theory of matter.

Felix (FEE licks) Roman governor of Alexandria, Egypt c. 130 A.D.

Felix, Mark Minucius (mark meh NEW shus FEE licks) *c. 130-215 A.D.* Roman lawyer who converted to Christianity. He wrote the apologetic work, *Octavius*.

Fundanus, Minucius (meh NEW shus fun DAN us) Roman proconsul of Asia c. 125 A.D.

Gallic (GAL ick) Pertaining to the people or province of Gaul.

Gauls (galls) The people who inhabited the Roman province of Gaul, which covered the modern-day countries of France and Belgium.

Granianus, Serenius (seh REN ee us GRA nee *ANN* us) Roman proconsul of Asia during the early second century.

Hadrian (HAY dree un) Roman emperor from 117 to 138 A.D. He suppressed the Jewish revolt led by Bar-Cochba.

Heraclitus (HAIR uh *KLI* tus) Greek philosopher of the 5th and 6th centuries B.C. He was known as the "weeping philosopher" because of his pessimistic view of life.

Hercules (HUR kyoo LEEZ) One of the sons of Zeus, known for his feats of strength.

Homer (HO mer) Ancient Greek poet, who probably lived around 850 B.C. Tradition credits him as the author of the epic poems, *Iliad* and *Odyssey*.

Hystaspes (hiss TASS peez) *c. 521 B.C.* Persian ruler and kinsman of Cyrus the Great.

Josephus, Flavius (FLAY vee us jo SEE fuss) *37-100 A.D.* Jewish historian of royal and priestly lineage. He was elected governor of Galilee by the Sanhedrin and took part in the Jewish revolt against the Romans in 66 A.D. He won pardon and favor from Emperor Vespasian. He wrote several important historical works including *History of the Jewish War* and *Antiquities of the Jews.*

Julianus, Antoninus (ANN teh NYE nuss JOOL ee *ANN* us) *100-169 A.D.* Preeminent Roman jurist and governor of Lower Germany under Emperor Antoninus Pius.

Jupiter (JOO peh ter) Rome's most important and powerful god. He was ruler over the other gods and was the god of the sky and thunder.

Jupiter Latiaris (JOO peh ter LAT ee *ARR* us) A title for Jupiter as god of the Latin League, a group of principalities in Italy. Solemn festivals were held annually on Mount Alban in Italy in honor of Jupiter Latiaris.

Justin Martyr (JUS tin MAR ter) *110-165 A.D.* Philosopher who converted to Christianity and became a tireless evangelist. His works are the earliest Christian apologies in existence. He was executed during the reign of Marcus Aurelius, about 165 A.D.

Magi (MAY ji) A priestly caste in Persia believed to have supernatural power.

Marcion (MAR she on *or* MAR see on) *110-165 A.D.* Prominent gnostic teacher of the second century who formed his own church and formulated his own New Testament.

Meander (mee ANN der) A first century gnostic disciple of Simon Magus. He claimed to be mankind's Savior and taught that men could deliver themselves through magic from the wicked angels who created the earth and held mankind captive.

Menander (mee NAN der) *343-291 B.C.* Greek poet and playwright who wrote more than 100 plays, known for their ingenious plots and wit.

Mercury (MURR kyoo ree) The messenger of the gods in Roman mythology.

Minerva (mih NERR vah) Roman goddess of wisdom and invention.

Minos (MI ness) A king of Crete, said in mythology to be a son of Jupiter and one of the three judges of the dead.

Mithras (MITH ras) The ancient Persian god of light and truth.

Octavius (ock TAY vee us) One of the three characters in *Octavius*. A devout Christian, he was Mark Felix's closest friend.

oracle (ORR eh kull) A person believed to be in communication with the gods; a prophet or prophetess.

Pegasus (PEG eh sus) A winged horse in Greek mythology.

Perseus (PURR soos *or* PURR see us) In Greek mythology, a son of Zeus and husband of Andromeda. He slew Medusa.

Phrygians (FRIDGE ee uns) The people of Phrygia, an ancient country located in modern day Turkey.

Pius, Antoninus (ANN teh NYE nuss PIE us) Roman emperor from 138-161 A.D. He succeeded Emperor Hadrian, his adoptive father, and enjoyed a long, prosperous reign. During his reign, the empire experienced no invasions or uprisings.

Plato (PLAY toe) *427-347 B.C.* Famous Greek philosopher who was a student of Socrates and teacher of Aristotle. He founded a school of philosophy known as the Academy, which eventually became the world's first university. He left numerous writings, most of which are in the form of dialogues.

Plautus (PLOW tus) A philosopher who, when in need, worked at a baker's hand mill.

Pompey (POM pee) *106-48 B.C.* Roman general and statesman. He was originally an ally of Julius Caesar, and he married Caesar's daughter, Julia. Later he became a bitter rival of Caesar.

Proserpina (pro SUR pee nuh) The Roman goddess who was the wife of Pluto, the god of the underworld.

Ptolemy II (TALL eh mee) *309-246 B.C.* Enlightened Grecian ruler of Egypt and Libya who encouraged literature and the arts. He commissioned the translation of the Greek Septuagint version.

Pythagoras (pih THAG o rus) *c. 550-500 B.C.* Greek philosopher and mathematician. He taught that earthly life is only a purification of the soul.

Romulus (ROMM you luss) The legendary founder of Rome, who killed his twin brother, Remus.

Saturn (SAT urn) The Roman god of agriculture.

Scaevola, Mucius (MYOO shuss SEE voe lah) *c. 509 B.C.* Roman hero who volunteered to assassinate Lars Porsena, who was beseiging Rome. His attempt failed, and he was told he would be burned alive unless he revealed all details of the assassination plot. Instead, he courageously stuck his right hand in a nearby fire, holding it there until it burned off. Because of his courage, his life was spared.

Serapis (seh RAY pis) A Roman god of the underworld.

sibyls (SIBB uhl) Any of a certain group of prophetesses or oracles of the Greeks and Romans. Many of their written prophecies speak of a coming Messiah. In their apologies, the early Christians pointed out these prophecies to the Romans. Some historians assume that the Christians altered the original Sibylline Books. Others think that the these books were Jewish in origin.

Simon Magus (SI munn MAY guess) First century Samaritan sorcerer described in Acts 8:9-24. He tried to purchase from Peter the power to impart the Holy Spirit to others. He later founded a heretical sect.

Simonides (sye MON eh DEEZ) A Greek poet of the fifth century B.C. who wrote many poems and hymns to the gods.

Socrates (SOCK reh teez) *470-399 B.C.* Famed philosopher and original thinker of Athens, Greece. His ideas and contempt for conventional ways brought him many enemies. He was condemned to death by the Athenian authorities and made to drink poison. Plato was his most famous pupil.

Sosthenes (SOSS then eez) Persian Magi who, centuries before Christ, wrote about the one true God and his angels.

Stoics (STOW icks) Members of a Greek school of philosophy founded around 380 B.C. They taught that all things are predestined by fate and that men should calmly accept the destiny determined for them.

Stygian (STIJ ee uhn) Pertaining to the River Styx and the underworld.

Ulysses (you LISS eez) King of the island of Ithaca, off the coast of Greece, and one of the Greek leaders of the Trojan War.

Venus (VEE nuss) Roman goddess of love, beauty, and spring.

Verus, Lucius (LOO shus VEER us) *130-169 A.D.* Adopted son of Emperor Antoninus Pius. He became co-ruler with Marcus Aurelius upon the death of Antoninus Pius.

Verus, Marcus Aurelius (MAR kus o REE lee us VEER us) *121-180 A.D.* Adopted son of Emperor Antoninus Pius. He ruled as the Roman Emperor from 161-180. He was very learned and was a respected Stoic philosopher, but as Emperor he severely persecuted the Christians.

Appendix One
Octavius

The chapter designations used in this book are those of the modern editor. The original work of Mark Felix was not divided into chapters. The translation of Dr. Robert Wallis, which was the basis of this rendition, numbered each paragraph as a separate chapter. The chapter designations used in this book correlate to those of Dr. Wallis as follows:

Chapter Designation Here	Dr. Wallis' Translation
1	1-4
2	5,13,6,7a,7c
3	8a,8c,9-12
4	14-16
5	17,18
6	24,25a,26b,27a,27c
7	28a,29,30,31
8	32,33,34,35,36a
9	36b-41

The following sections were omitted from the text of *Octavius* as presented here. The chapter numbers below are as they are designated in Dr. Wallis' translation.

From Caecilius' Speech

Chap. 7b.

"Witness the Idaean mother, who at her arrival both approved the chastity of the matron, and delivered the city from the fear of the enemy. Witness the statues of the equestrian brothers, consecrated even as they had showed themselves on the lake, who, with horses breathless, foaming, and smoking, announced the victory over the Persian on the same day on which they had gained it. Witness the renewal of the games of the offended Jupiter, on account of the dream of a man of the people. The devotion of the Decii is another acknowledged witness. Look also at Curtius, who filled up the opening of the profound chasm either with the mass, or with the glory of his knighthood. Moreover, more frequently than we wished have the auguries, when despised, borne witness to the presence of the gods; thus Allia is an unlucky name; thus the battle of Claudius and Junius is not a battle against the Carthaginians, but a fatal shipwreck. Thus, that Thrasymenus might be both swollen and discolored with the blood of the Romans, Flaminius despised the auguries; and that we might again demand our standards from the Parthians, Crassus both deserved and scoffed at the imprecations of the terrible sisters. I omit the old stories, which are many, and I pass by the songs of the poets about the births, and the gifts, and the rewards of the gods. Moreover, I hasten over the fates predicted by the oracles, lest antiquity should appear to you excessively fabulous."

Chap. 8b.

"Theodorus of Cyrene, or one who is before him, Diagoras the Melian, to whom antiquity applied the surname of Atheist—both of whom, by asserting that there were no gods, took away all the fear by which humanity is ruled, and all veneration absolutely; yet never will they prevail in this discipline of impiety, under the name and authority of their pretended philosophy."

From Octavius' Speech

Chap. 19.

"I hear that the poets also speak of 'the One Father of gods and men' and that such is the mind of mortal men as the Parent of all has appointed His day. Notice too what the Mantuan Maro says. His words are even more plain and true. He says, 'In the beginning the spirit within nourishes, and the mind infused stirs the heaven and the earth,' and the other members 'of the world. And from there arises the race of men and of cattle,' and every other kind of animal. In another place, this same poet says that this mind and spirit is actually God. In fact, his very words are: 'This God pervades all the lands and sea, and the very heavens. All men and cattle come from him, as does the rain and fire.' And don't we ourselves teach that our God is mind, reason, and spirit?

"Let me also review the teachings of the philosophers. Although they spoke of many diverse things, they all agreed on one matter. I'm going to pass over the untrained and ancient ones who deserved to be called wise men for their teachings. And I will start with Thales the Milesian, for he was the first to expound about heavenly things. He taught that water was the beginning of all things, but that God was the mind from which the water was able to create all things. Ah! A higher and nobler account of water and spirit than any humans had spoken. So his thoughts must have been given him by God. For the opinion of this original philosopher absolutely agrees with ours.

"Later, Anaximenes, and then Diogenes of Apollonia, taught that the air, infinite and unmeasured, is God. Their views of Divinity are also like ours. Anaxagoras also said that God is the motion of an infinite mind. And Pythagoras taught that God is the soul passing to and fro throughout the universal nature of things. He also said that this God gave life to all creatures. Another philosopher, Xenophanes, taught that God is all infinity with a mind. Antisthenes said that although there are many gods of the people, there is one God of Nature who is the chief of all. Xeuxippus taught that God is a natural animal force that governs all things.

"How about Democritus? Although he was the first to speak of atoms, he also said that Nature, the basis of forms and intelligence, is God. Strato, too, said that God is Nature. Even Epicurus, who said that there were either no gods or else only useless ones, still admitted that Nature was over all. Aristotle wavers on this matter, but he still taught a unity of power. At one time he said that Mind is God; another time he said the World is God. Still another, he said that God is above the world. Heraclides of Pontus also ascribed, although in various ways, a Divine Mind to God.

"Theophrastus, Zeno, Chrysippus, and Cleanthes expressed different opinions about God. But they all came to the same conclusion: there is a unity of Providence. Cleanthes sometimes talked of God as of a mind, then of a soul, other times of air, but most of the time as of reason. Zeno, his master, said the law of nature and of God—and sometimes air and reason—is the beginning of all things. Moreover, by interpreting Juno to be the air, Jupiter the heaven, Neptune the sea, Vulcan the fire, and the other gods to be various elements of nature, he forcibly denounced and overturned the public error. Chrysippus said almost the same thing. He believed that a Divine force, a rational nature, fatal necessity, and sometimes the world to be God. And he followed the example of Zeno in his physiological interpretation of the poems of Hesiod, of Homer, and of Orpheus.

"Moreover, the teaching of Diogenes of Babylon is that of expounding and arguing that the birth of Jupiter, and the origin of Minerva, and this kind, are names for other things, not for gods. Xenophon the Socratic said that the form of the true God cannot be seen, and therefore ought not to be inquired after. Aristo the Stoic said that God cannot at all be comprehended. So both of them were cognizant of the majesty of God, while they both despaired of understanding him.

"Plato had a clearer understanding of God—both as to terminology and factual matters themselves. In fact, his teachings would be altogether heavenly if he had not occasionally polluted them by a mixture of opinions about mere civil matters. For example, in *Timaeus*, Plato's God is by his very name the Parent of the world, the Creator of the soul, the Maker of heaven and earth. Plato said that God was difficult to discover because of his incredible power, and that once you have discovered him, it's impossible to speak about him in public. Our beliefs are almost the same. For we both know and speak of a God who is the Parent of all. And we never speak of him in public unless we are interrogated." [Ed. note: At the time of this discussion, Christianity was an outlawed religion.]

Chap. 20

"I have set forth the opinions of almost all of the philosophers whose illustrious glory it was to have pointed out that there is only one God, although they ascribed different names to him. So a person might suppose that either Christians are philosophers, or that the philosophers were Christians.

"But if the universe is governed by Providence, and directed by the will of one God, we should not be carried away by the erroneous opinions of the ancients. Even if we are charmed by the fables of old. For these fables are rebutted by the opinions of the philosophers, who have the support of reason—as well as antiquity. For our ancestors were gullible. They even believed in all sorts of monsters as being marvelous wonders, such as a Scylla, a multi-formed Chimera, a Hydra of many heads that grew again when cut off, and creatures called Centaurs, who were a combination of horse and man.

"In fact, they were willing to listen to whatever stories were conjured up. Why should I go on about such old wives' tales, such as men turning into birds, beasts, trees, and flowers? If such things had really happened in the past, they would also happen again. And because they can't happen now shows they never happened at all. Similarly, with respect to the gods, our ancestors believed things too gullibly and indiscriminately. They worshipped their kings religiously, and after their deaths, they preserved their memories in statues. Although such statues were originally made as a memorial, they soon were viewed as something sacred. So before there was much commerce between nations, which caused various customs and religions to be intermingled, each nation venerated its founder, or illustrious hero, or modest queen braver than her sex, or discoverer of art or inventions. And thus a monument was given to the deceased, which served as an example of those who were to follow."

Chap. 21.

"Read the writings of the Stoics, or the writings of other wise men, so you can verify that these matters are true. Euhemerus said that men were esteemed gods because of their virtue or of some gift. He even enumerated the dates of birth, homelands, and places of burial of many of the so-called gods. For example, he lists such information about the Dictaean Jupiter, the Delphic Apollo, the Pharian Isis, and the Eleusinian Ceres.

"Prodicus spoke of men who were taken up among the gods, because they discovered new types of food crops as a result of their travels and thus helped their fellowmen. Persaeus said the same thing. He even names the plants and fruits discovered by such travelers, and he shows that those persons were eventually called by the name of the plant discovered. As the passage of the comic writer runs, Venus freezes without Bacchus and Ceres.

"Alexander the Great, the celebrated Macedonian, wrote in a remarkable document addressed to his mother, that out of fear of Alexander, a priest had confessed to him that the gods were really men. He told his mother that Vulcan was the first of all, and then the race of Jupiter.

"And you behold the swallow and the cymbal of Isis, and the tomb of your Serapis or Osiris empty, with his limbs scattered about. Then consider the sacred rites themselves and their very mysteries. You will find mournful deaths, misfortunes, funerals, and the griefs and wailings of the miserable gods. Isis laments, seeking her lost son. With her are Cynocephalus and her bald priests. The wretched worshippers of Isis beat their breasts and imitate the grief of Isis, this unhappy mother. But by and by the little boy is found, and Isis and her companions rejoice. So the ritual goes on year after year. They forever lose what they find or find what they lose. Isn't it ridiculous either to grieve over what you worship, or to worship that which you grieve over? Although these were formerly Egyptian rites, now they're Roman ones as well.

"Ceres, entwined with a serpent, torch in hand, anxiously tracks the footprints of Proserpine, who was abducted and corrupted. These are the Eleusinian mysteries. And what are the sacred rites of Jupiter? His nurse is a she-goat, and as an infant he is taken away from his greedy father, lest he should be devoured. And the worshippers crash cymbals loudly so that the father won't hear the baby's crying. I am ashamed to even mention the rites of Cybele of Dindymus. She, being the mother of the gods, was old and ugly, and couldn't entice her adulterous lover to lewdness. And so she had him made into a eunuch, no doubt so that she could make a god of the eunuch. Because of this fable, the Gauls worship her by the punishment of their emasculated bodies. But all these things are not sacred rites—they're tortures.

"Think about the very forms and appearances of the gods? Don't your very statues evidence the contemptible and disgraceful characters of your gods? Vulcan is a lame and crippled god. Apollo is portrayed as still smooth-faced despite his advanced age, while his son, Aesculapius, is full bearded. Neptune has sea-green eyes; Minerva, blue-grey ones; and Juno, the eyes of an ox. Mercury has winged feet; Pan, hoofed feet; and Saturn, chained feet. Janus is portrayed as having two faces, so that he can walk forward and still look behind as he goes. Diana sometimes is shown as a huntress, with her robe girded up high. As the goddess of the Ephesians, she has many and fruitful breasts. When portrayed as Trivia, she is represented as a horrible creature with three heads and many hands.

"Think of your statues of Jupiter. Some images show him as beardless; others, bearded. When called by the name Hammon, he is represented with horns. When Capitolinus, he wields thunderbolts. When Latiaris, he is sprinkled with blood. I could go on and on about the various representations of Jupiter. His monstrous appearances are as numerous as his names.

"Erigone was hanged from a noose, that as a virgin she might shine among the stars. The Castors die by turns, that they may live. Aesculapius is struck with a thunderbolt so that he can rise into a god. Hercules is burned up by the fires of Oeta, so that he can shed his humanity."

Chap. 22.

"Not only do we learn these fables and errors from our ignorant parents, but even worse, we enlarge them in our studies and writings. This is particularly true in the writings of the poets. Through their authority, they have prejudiced the truth as much as possible. It is for this reason that Plato expelled the illustrious Homer, whom he had praised and crowned, from the imaginary idealistic state created in his discourse. For in his writings about the Trojan war, Homer portrayed the gods as interfering in the affairs of men, although Homer made jests of the gods. He portrayed the gods as being brought together in battle. He wounded Venus. He not only wounded Mars, but also had him bound and driven away. He related that Jupiter was set free by Briareus, so as not to be bound fast by the rest of the gods. He told of Jupiter bewailing with showers of blood the death of his son Sarpedon, for he could not save him from death. He also wrote of Jupiter being enticed by the girdle of Venus and as a result thereof laying more eagerly with his wife Juno than he was accustomed to do with his adulterous loves.

"Elsewhere, Hercules threw out dung, and Apollo fed the cattle for Admetus. Neptune built walls for Laomedon, but the unfortunate builder didn't receive his wages for his work. Homer spoke of Aeneas forging the thunderbolt of Jupiter on an anvil. But there were heaven, lightning, and thunderbolts long before Jupiter was born in Crete. The Cyclops cannot imitate, nor can Jupiter help but fear, the flames of the real thunderbolt. Why should I speak of the detected adultery of Mars and Venus? Or of the violence of Jupiter against Ganymede—a deed supposedly consecrated in heaven?

"The real reason these myths have been fabricated is to give authority for the vices of humans. These fables corrupt the minds of boys and cling to them as they grow to manhood. They still believe these things when they're old men, even though the truth is plain if they will only seek after it. For the ancient writers reveal that Saturn, the author of this race, was a man. Nepos knew this. Cassius spoke of it in his histories. Thallus and Diodorus said the same thing. This Saturn, driven from Crete by the fear of his raging son, then fled to Italy, where he was hospitably received by Janus. Being learned and of a Greek-related people, he taught the unskilled and rustic Italians many things. For example, he taught them how to write, coin money, and make instruments. He chose the name Latium, which means hidden, for his new-found place of refuge. And he named a city Saturnia after himself. Like Saturn, Janus left his name to the memory of posterity by naming a city after himself—Janiculum.

"So Saturn was simply a man—a man who fled, who was given refuge, who was born of an earthly father, and who himself was the father of children. But among the Italians, he was of unknown parents. So they said he was born of heaven, or that he sprung from the earth. Just like today, we often say that someone who appears unexpectedly is 'sent from heaven.' Or that those who are of lowly condition and unknown are 'sons of the earth.' After Saturn was driven out of Crete, his son Jupiter reigned in Crete. He fathered sons and eventually died there in Crete. In fact, to this day people visit the cave of Jupiter and see his coffin. These very rites prove that he was merely human."

Chap. 23

"I could go on about the origin of other gods, but it is pointless. Since Saturn and Jupiter are deemed to be the fathers of the other gods, their descendants were obviously human just as they were. Unless you want to claim that they became gods after their deaths. Romulus became a god through the perjury of Proculus. Juba became a god through the good will of the Mauritanians. Other kings have been declared gods, not so much because their subjects truly believed in their divinity, but because they feared the power of their kings.

"Ironically, the kings themselves are in no hurry to become gods. They would rather continue to live in their human condition than to be deified upon their deaths. Although they may be old men, they do not seek godhood. But real gods are not made from dead people. For a god cannot die. Neither are they made from those who are born, for everyone who is born eventually dies. But he is truly Divine who neither is born nor dies.

"If gods were really born in times past, why aren't they still born today? Could it be that Jupiter has grown too old? Or that Juno is beyond the age of childbearing? Has Minerva grown gray before she has had any children? Or is the truth simply that people would no longer believe such fables of godhood and so no new gods have come to life? Furthermore, if the gods could create, they could not perish. The result is that there would be more gods than humans. Neither the heavens, the air, or the earth could contain them. So again it's obvious that those gods we read about as having been born and having died are simply humans.

"Therefore, who can deny that the common people pray to and publicly worship the images of these men? The sensibilities of the ignorant are deceived by the artist's skill. They're blinded by the glittering of gold, the shimmering of silver, or the whiteness of ivory. But if anyone really thought about how images are made and the tools that made them, he would blush with embarrassment that he had ever feared mere stone, metal, or wood that had been shaped by a craftsman into a god.

"For example, to make a wooden god, the craftsman selects an ordinary log, hangs it up, and then cuts, hews, and planes it. To make a god of brass or silver, the craftsman often takes used ordinary utensils, such as a footbath (as did one Egyptian king), and then beats, hammers, and forges it on an anvil. Similarly, a god of stone is cut, sculptured, and polished. The god no more feels the worship given it then it feels the hammering and cutting that made it.

"If you say, 'The rough materials are not yet a god,' then when does the god come into existence? Look! It is melted, wrought, and sculptured—but it isn't a god yet. Look! It is soldered, shaped, and set up—but still it isn't a god. Look! Now it is worshipped, consecrated, and prayed to. So does it suddenly now become a god? If so, then it only becomes a god when man chooses it to become one."

Chap. 25b

"We know about the native gods of the Romans—Romulus, Picus, Tiberinus, Consus, Pilumnus, and Picumnus. Tatius both discovered and worshipped Cloacina [sewer], Hostilius, Fear, and Palor. A god named Fever was later dedicated by I don't know whom. Such were the types of superstition that pervaded Rome—diseases and ill states of health. Acca Laurentia and Flora, infamous prostitutes, can also be included among these diseases that became gods for the Romans. No doubt it was such gods that enabled the Romans to enlarge their empire. No doubt such Roman gods prevailed against those gods worshipped by the other nations. For the gods of the nations did not help their own worshippers against the Romans. Such gods as the Thracian Mars; the Cretan Jupiter; Juno of Argos, Samos, and Carthage; Diana of Tauris; the Idaean Mother; and the Egyptian gods were useless. They aren't deities, but monstrosities.

"But perhaps the chastity of virgins was greater among the Romans, or the religion of the priests more holy. Yet, we all know that among many of the vestal virgins, *unchastity* was punished, in that they—doubtless without the knowledge of Vesta—had sexual relations too carelessly with men. And for the rest, their impunity arose not from the better protection of their chastity, but from the better fortune of their immodesty. And where are adulteries better arranged by the priests than among the very altars and shrines? Where are more sexual encounters made, or more acts of violence concerted? In fact, burning lust is more often gratified in the little chambers of the temple keepers than in the brothels themselves.

"Yet, long before the Romans, by the ordering of the real God, the Assyrians held dominion. So did the Medes and Persians, the Greeks and the Egyptians. Yet, they had no Pontiffs, nor Arvales, nor Salii, nor vestal virgins, nor Augurs. Neither did they have chickens penned up in a coop, by whose feeding or abstinence the highest concerns of the state were to be governed."

Chap. 26a

"Now let me address the omens and fortunetellers you Romans have collected with such extreme care. You've testified that good fortune followed the careful observance of such things. And that ill consequences followed the neglect of them. No doubt Clodius, Flaminius, and Junius lost their armies on this account—that they did not consider it worthwhile to wait for the very solemn omen given by the hungry pecking of the chickens. But what of Regulus? He took care to observe the omens, but he was still captured, wasn't he? Mancinus, also, followed the prescribed religious rites and yet was enslaved. Paulus also had hungry chickens at Cannae, yet he was overthrown along with the greater part of the Republic.

"Caius Caesar paid no attention to the omens and soothsayers that told him he should not take his army into Africa before the winter. But by ignoring them, his journey was made much easier and he still conquered. What more shall I say about such omens? After his death, Amphiaraus supposedly was able to communicate about future events. Strangely, when living he didn't know that his wife was about to betray him because of a bracelet. The blind Tiresias was supposed to see the future, but he couldn't even see the present. Ennius invented the replies of the Pythian Apollo concerning Pyrrhus, although Apollo had already ceased to make verses. How suspicious that his cautious and ambiguous oracle failed just at the time when men began to be more cultured and less gullible. And Demosthenes, because he knew that the answers were feigned, complained that the Pythia philippized."

Chap. 27b.

"These raging maniacs also, whom you see rush about in public, are moreover themselves prophets without a temple; thus they rage, thus they rave, thus they are whirled around. In them also there is a like instigation of the demon, but there is a dissimilar occasion for their madness. From the same causes also arise those things which were spoken of a little time ago by you, that Jupiter demanded the restoration of his games in a dream, that the Castors appeared with horses, and that a small ship was following the leading of the matron's girdle."

Chap. 28b.

"When, if reason and not the instigation of a demon were to judge, they should rather have been pressed not to disavow themselves Christians, but to confess themselves guilty of incests, of abominations, of sacred rites polluted, of infants immolated. For with these and such as these stories, did those same demons fill up the ears of the ignorant against us, to the horror of their execration. Nor yet was it wonderful, since the common report of men, which is always fed by the scattering of falsehoods, is wasted away when the truth is brought to light. Thus, this is the business of demons, for by them false rumors are both sown and cherished.

"Thence arises what you say that you hear, that an ass's head is esteemed among us a divine thing. Who is such a fool as to worship this? Who is so much more foolish as to believe that it is an object of worship? Unless that you even consecrate whole asses in your stables, together with your Epona, and religiously devour those same asses with Isis. Also you offer up and worship the heads of oxen and of wethered goats, and you dedicate gods mingled also of a goat and a man, and gods with the faces of dogs and lions. Do you not adore and feed Apis the ox, with the Egyptians? And you do not condemn their sacred rites instituted in honor of serpents, and crocodiles, and other beasts, and birds, and fishes, of which if any one were to kill one of these gods, he is even punished with death. These same Egyptians, together with very many of you, are not more afraid of Isis than they are of the pungency of onions, nor of Serapis more than they tremble at the basest noises produced by the foulness of their bodies. He also who fables against us about our adoration of the members of the priest, tries to confer upon us what belongs really to himself. [Ed. note: Dr. Wallis left the following sentence untranslated: Ista enim impudicitiae eorum forsitan sacra sint, apud quos sexus omnis membris omnibus prostat, apud quos tota impudicitia vocatur urbanitas; qui scortorum licentiae invident, qui medios viros lambunt, libidinoso ore inguinibus inhaerescunt, homines malae lingue etiam si tacerent, quos prius taedescit impudicitiae suae quam pudescit.] Abomination! They suffer on themselves such evil deeds, as no age is so effeminate as to be able to bear, and no slavery so cruel as to be compelled to endure."

Omitted Sentences

The following sentences were omitted from Caecilius' speech:

"Hence the perpetual course of their veneration has continued, which is not weakened by the long lapse of time, but increased, because antiquity has been accustomed to attribute to ceremonies and temples so much of sanctity as it has ascribed of age." (Ch. 6) "Nor yet by chance (for I would venture in the meantime even to take for granted the point in debate, and so to err on the safe side) have our ancestors succeeded in their undertakings either by the observance of auguries, or by consulting the entrails, or by the institution of sacred rites, or by the dedication of temples." (Ch. 7) "So does a deceitful hope soothe their fear with the solace of a revival." (Ch. 8) "From this source flowed the safe doubting of Arcesilas, and long after of Carneades, and of very many of the Academics, in questions of the highest moment, in which species of philosophy the unlearned can do much with caution, and the learned can do gloriously. What! Is not the hesitation of Simonides the lyric poet to be admired and followed by all?" (Ch. 13)

The following sentences were omitted from Octavius' speech:

"Thus avarice has been consecrated in gold and silver; thus the form of empty statues has been established; thus has arisen Roman superstition." (Ch. 24) "As often, therefore, as the Romans triumphed, so often they were polluted; and as many trophies as they gained from the nations, so many spoils did they take from the gods." (Ch. 25) "For neither were the Romans able in the wars themselves to have the help of the gods against whom they took up arms; and they began to worship those when they were triumphed over, whom they had previously challenged." (Ch. 25) "Now these spirits, after having lost the simplicity of their nature by being weighed down and immersed in vices, for a solace of their calamity, cease not, now that they are ruined themselves, to ruin others; and being depraved themselves, to infuse into others the error of their depravity." (Ch. 26) "By their [the demons'] aspirations and communications the Magi show their wondrous tricks, making either those things appear which are not, or those things not to appear which are." (Ch. 26) "And Sosthenes knew that it enhanced his veneration, that in awe of the very nod and glance of their Lord they should tremble." (Ch. 26)

"Whence also Plato warns us of the desire of love, and he says that it is moulded and glides into the human breast, and stirs the senses, and moulds the affections, and infuses the ardor of lust." (Ch. 26) "Inasmuch as the demons are ignorant of the simple truth, and for their own ruin they don't confess that which they know." (Ch. 27) "They disturb the life and render all men unquiet." (Ch. 27) "The demons constrain men to worship them, being gorged with the fumes of altars or the sacrifices of cattle." (Ch. 27) "These, and such as these infamous things, we are not at liberty even to hear. It is even disgraceful with any more words to defend ourselves from such charges. For you pretend that those things are done by chaste and modest persons, which we should not believe to be done at all, unless you proved that they were true concerning yourselves." (Ch. 29)

"And what is worthy of the son of Saturn, he is gorged with the blood of an evil and criminal man. I believe that he himself taught Catiline to conspire under a compact of blood, and Bellona to steep her sacred rites with a draught of human gore." (Ch. 30) "It was thus your own Fronto acted in this respect: he did not produce testimony, as one who alleged a charge, but he scattered reproaches as a rhetorician." (Ch. 31) "It is ungrateful when the victim fit for sacrifice is a good disposition, and a pure mind, and a sincere judgment." (Ch. 32) "Thus it is no wonder if that mass [the earth] be destroyed by him who created it." (Ch. 34) "Yet I will speak according as I feel. No one can be so poor as he is born." (Ch. 36)

Appendix Two
Justin's First Apology

The chapter designations used in this book are those of the modern editor. The original work of Justin Martyr was not divided into chapters. The translation of Dr. Dods, which was the basis of this rendition, numbered each paragraph as a separate chapter. As was mentioned in the introduction, the modern editor has rearranged the order of Justin's paragraphs so that his thoughts flow in logical sequence. The chapter designations used in this book correlate to those of Dr. Dods as follows:

Chapter Designation Here	Translation of Dr. Dods
1	1,2,3,4
2	11,12a,8a,14a,14b(excerpt)
3	14b,15a,27,29,15b,16a,17a,7, 16b,12b
4	17b,18,19,57,27b(excerpt), 28,8b(excerpt)
5	61
6	65,66,67
7	5,25,6,9,10,13
8	46,26,58b,64,62,55
9	63
10	8b,20,21,22,59,60,23,24
11	30,31,32,33
12	34,35,39,40a,45,47,48a,49a, 53b,53a,53c,52
13	43,44
14	68

Although this rendition was taken from the translation of Dr. Dods, on obscure passages the editor has sometimes consulted the translation edited by Dr. Cyril C. Richardson, which is included in a volume entitled *Early Christian Fathers*, published by Macmillan Publishing Co. In order to condense Justin's apology, the following chapters (as numbered in Dr. Dods' translation) were omitted from the main text, but have been reproduced here.

Chap. 36

But when you hear the prophets speaking in first person, you should not think that they were speaking of their own accord. Rather they spoke as the Divine Logos moved them. For sometimes the Logos spoke in the manner of a prophet, foretelling things that were to come. Other times he spoke as from the person of God himself, the Lord and Father of all. Sometimes he spoke in the person of Christ. Other times, he spoke in the voice of the people answering Christ, or answering Christ's Father. This manner of writing should not seem unusual, for many of your writings are similar. Each book has only one author, but he speaks through various persons in the dialogue. However, the Jews did not understand this manner of writing, and as a result they did not recognize Christ when he came. Instead, they hate us for saying that Christ has come and for saying that they crucified him, as was predicted.

Chap. 37

For example, through the prophet Isaiah, the following words were spoken in the person of the Father: "The ox knows his owner; the donkey knows his master's crib. But Israel does not know, and my people have not understood. Woe to you, sinful nation, a people full of sins. You are a wicked seed, children that are lawbreakers. You have forsaken the Lord." [Isa. 1:3] Again, the same prophet speaks in the voice of the Father: "What is the house that you will build for me? says the Lord. The heaven is my throne, and the earth is my footstool." [Isa. 66:1] "Your new moons and your sabbaths my soul hates. I cannot bear the great day of the fast and of ceasing from labor. Even if you come to be seen of me, I will not hear you. Your hands are full of blood. If you bring fine flour or incense, it is an abomination to me. The fat of lambs and the blood of bulls I do not desire. For who has required this from your hands. But loosen every bond of wickedness. Tear asunder the tight knots of violent contracts. Shelter the homeless and naked. Give bread to the hungry." [Isa. 1:14; 58:6,7]

This will give you an idea of the types of things that are spoken through the prophets in the person of God.

Chap. 38

Here are some examples of the Spirit of prophecy speaking in the person of Christ: "I have spread out my hands to a disobedient and obstinate people, to those who walk in a way that is not good." [Isa. 65:2] And again, "I gave my back to the whips and my cheeks to the buffetings. I did not turn my face away from the shame of spittings. The Lord was my helper. Therefore, I was not confounded. But I set my face as a firm rock. I knew that I should not be ashamed, for he is near who justifies me." [Isa. 50:6] Another example is: "They cast lots for my clothes and pierced my hands and feet. I lay down and slept, and rose again, for the Lord sustained me." [Ps. 22:18; 3:5]

And all of those things actually happened to Christ at the hands of the Jews, which you can verify. For when he was crucified, they mocked him and shook their heads, saying, "Let him who raised the dead save himself." [Luke 23:35]

Chap. 40b

I feel it would be worthwhile to mention some of the other prophecies of David. From these you can learn how the Spirit of prophecy exhorts men to live. You can learn how he foretold the conspiracy against Christ by Herod (king of the Jews), Pontius Pilate (governor of Judea), Pilate's soldiers, and the Jews themselves. And there are even more things to learn. How men of every nation would believe in Christ. How God declares Christ to be his Son. How God has said that he will subdue all of his enemies under Christ. How the demons, to the best of their ability, try to escape the power of God, the Father and Lord of all, and the power of Christ himself. And finally, how God calls all people to repentance before his day of judgment comes.

All of these things were foretold in the following prophecy of David: "Blessed is the man who has not walked in the counsel of the ungodly, nor stood in the way of sinners, nor sat in the seat of the scornful. But his delight is in the law of the Lord. In his law he will meditate day and night. And he shall be like a tree planted by the rivers of waters, which shall give his fruit in his season. His leaf shall not wither, and whatever he does shall prosper. But it is not so for the ungodly, who are like the chaff which the wind drives away from the face of the earth. Therefore, the ungodly will not stand in the judgment, nor sinners in the council of the righteous. For the Lord knows the way of the righteous. But the way of the ungodly shall perish. Why do the heathens rage and the people imagine new things? The kings of the earth set themselves, and the rulers take counsel together against the Lord and against his Christ, saying 'Let us break their bands asunder and cast their yoke from us.' He that dwells in the heavens shall laugh at them, and the Lord shall have them in derision. He shall speak to them in his wrath and vex them in his sore pleasure. Yet I have been set by him as a king on Zion his holy mountain, declaring the decree of the Lord. The Lord said to me, 'You are my Son. This day I have begotten you.' Ask of me, and I shall give you the heathen for your inheritance and the uttermost parts of the earth as your possession. You shall harm them with a rod of iron. You will dash them in pieces as the vessels of a potter. Be wise now O you kings. Be instructed, all you judges of the earth. Serve the Lord with fear and rejoice with trembling. Embrace instruction lest the Lord be angry and you perish from the right way when his wrath is kindled. Blessed are all they that put their trust in him" [Ps. 1:1-6;2:1-10].

Chap. 41

And again, in another prophecy, the Spirit of prophecy, through the same David, implied that Christ, after he had been crucified, would reign, and spoke as follows: "Sing to the Lord, all the earth, and day by day declare his salvation. For great is the Lord, and greatly to be praised, to be feared above all the gods. For all the gods of the nations are idols of devils. But God made the heavens. Glory and praise are before his face. Strength and glorying are in the dwelling of his holiness. Give glory to the Lord, the Father everlasting. Receive grace, and enter his presence, and worship in his holy courts. Let all the earth fear before his face; let it be established, and not shaken. Let them rejoice among the nations. The Lord has reigned from the tree." [Ps. 96:1-10]

Chap. 42

But the Spirit of prophecy speaks of things that are about to come to pass as if they had already taken place. This may be observed in the passages already cited by me. That this circumstance may afford no excuse to readers [for misinterpreting them], we will make even this also quite plain. The things that God absolutely knows will take place, he predicts as if already they had taken place. And that the utterances must be thus received, you will perceive, if you give your attention to them. The words cited above, David uttered 1500 years before Christ became a man and was crucified. And nobody who lived before him, and none of his contemporaries, gave joy to the Gentiles by being crucified. But our Jesus Christ, being crucified and dead, rose again, and having ascended to heaven, reigned. And by those things which were declared in his name among all nations by the apostles, there is joy given to those who expect the immortality promised by him.

Chap. 48b

Isaiah also prophesied that Christ, and those who believed in him, would be killed: "Behold now the righteous perish, and no man lays it to heart. Just men are taken away, and no one considers it. The righteous man is taken away from the presence of wickedness. His burial shall be in peace. He is taken from our midst" [Isa. 57:1,2].

Chap. 49b

It was foreknown that people would speak lies against those who confess Christ. And Isaiah foretold that those slanderers, who say it is better to hold to the ancient customs, would be punished, saying, "Woe to those who call sweet bitter, and bitter sweet" [Isa. 5:20].

Chap. 50.

Having become man for our sake, Christ willingly suffered and accepted humiliation. But he will come again with glory, as the following prophecies show: "Because they delivered his soul unto death, and he was counted among the evildoers, he has carried the sins of many. He shall make intercession for the transgressors. For behold, my servant shall deal prudently, and he shall be exalted and greatly praised. As many were astonished at you, so disfigured shall your form be before men, and so hidden from them your glory. Likewise, many nations shall wonder, and the kings shall shut their mouths at him. For they to whom it was not told, and they who have not heard, shall understand. Oh, Lord, who has believed our report? To whom is the arm of the Lord revealed? We brought a report as of a child before him, as a root in dry ground. He had no form or glory. We saw him and there was no form or comeliness. But his form was dishonored and marred more than the sons of men. A man under the stroke, and knowing how to bear infirmity, because his face was turned away. He was despised and of no reputation. It is he who bears our sins and is afflicted for us. Yet we did esteem him smitten, stricken, and afflicted. But he was wounded for our transgressions. He was bruised for our iniquities, the chastisement of peace was upon him. By his stripes we are healed. All we, like sheep, have gone astray. Every man has wandered in his own way. And he delivered him for our sins. He opened not his mouth for all his affliction. He was brought as a sheep to the slaughter. As a lamb before his shearer is dumb, so he did not open his mouth. In his humiliation, his judgment was taken away." [Isa. 52:13-15; 53:1-8]

As was prophesied, after Jesus was crucified, even his companions abandoned him, having denied him. Afterwards, when Jesus had risen from the dead and appeared to them, he showed them the prophecies that foretold all those things to happen. And when they had seen him ascending into heaven, they believed in him and received the power sent by him to them. They were called apostles and went out to every nation of men and taught these things.

Chap. 51.

The Spirit of prophecy signified that the person who suffered these things would have an indescribable origin. He also foretold that this person would rule over his enemies. The Spirit said, "Who shall declare his generation? Because his life is cut off from the earth, for their transgressions he comes to death. I will give the wicked for his burial and the rich for his death. Because he did no violence, neither was any deceit found in his mouth. The Lord is pleased to cleanse him from the stripe. If he is given for sin, your soul shall see his seed prolonged in days. The Lord is pleased to deliver his soul from grief, to show him light, and to form him with knowledge, to justify the righteous who richly serve many. And he shall bear our sins. Therefore, he shall inherit many, and he shall divide the spoil of the strong because his soul was delivered to death. And he was numbered among the transgressors. And he bore the sins of many, and he was delivered up for their transgressions." [Isa. 53:8-12]

Hear, too, how he was to ascend into heaven according to the prophecy: "Lift up the gates of heaven. Be opened, that the king of glory may come in. Who is the king of glory? The Lord, strong and mighty." [Ps. 24:7] The prophet Jeremiah foretold how he would come again from heaven in glory, saying, "Behold, as the son of man he comes in the clouds of heaven, together with his angels." [Dan. 7:13]

Chap. 54

But those who hand down the myths which the poets have made furnish no proof to the youths who learn them. And I will demonstrate that they have been uttered by the influence of the wicked demons, to deceive and mislead the human race. For they heard the prophecies that the Christ was to come, and that the ungodly among men were to be punished by fire. So they put forward the so-called sons of Jupiter, under the impression that they would be able to produce in men the idea that the things which were said about Christ were simply mythical stories, like those told by the poets. And these things were said both among the Greeks and among all nations where the demons heard the prophets foretelling that Christ would specially be believed in. However, I will make plain that they did not accurately understand what was said by the prophets. So they erroneously imitated what was said about our Christ. As I have already said, the prophet Moses was older than all writers. And by him, as I have also said, it was predicted: "There shall not fail a prince from Judah, nor a lawgiver from between his feet, until he comes for whom it is reserved. And he shall be the desire of the Gentiles, binding his foal to the vine, washing his robe in the blood of the grape" [Gen. 49:10]. When they heard these prophetic words, the devils said that Bacchus was the son of Jupiter. And they proclaimed that he was the discoverer of the vine. For that reason, they include wine among his mysteries. And they taught that Bacchus was torn into pieces and that he then ascended into heaven.

However, the prophecy of Moses did not expressly state whether he who was to come was the Son of God [or the son of man]. Nor did it state whether he would, riding on the foal, remain on earth or ascend into heaven. Also, the word "foal" could mean either the offspring of a donkey or the offspring of a horse. So the devils did not know whether he who was foretold would bring the foal of a donkey or that of a horse as the sign of his coming. And they didn't know whether he was the Son of God, or the son of man. So they said that Bellerophon, a man born of man, ascended to heaven on his horse Pegasus.

And when they heard it said by the other prophet, Isaiah, that he should be born of a virgin, and by his own means would ascend into heaven, they pretended that Perseus was being spoken of. And they also knew that the prophecies foretold that he would be 'strong as a giant to run his course.' [Ps. 19:5] So they said that Hercules was strong, and that he had journeyed over the whole earth. Likewise, they learned that it had been foretold that he would heal every sickness and raise the dead. So they produced Aesculapius.

Chap. 58a

And, as we said before, the devils put forward Marcion of Pontus, who is even now teaching men to deny that God is the maker of all things in heaven and on earth, and that the Christ predicted by the prophets is his Son, and preaches another god besides the Creator of all, and likewise another son. And many have believed this man, as if he alone knew the truth. They laugh at us, although they have no proof of what they say. So they are carried away irrationally as lambs by a wolf, and become the prey of atheistic doctrines, and of devils.

Omitted Sentences:

The following sentences were omitted from the main text in this rendition:

"And, indeed, so far at least as one may judge from the name we are accused of, we are most excellent people. But we do not think it just to be acquitted on account of the name if we are convicted as criminals." (Ch. 2) "So far as our name goes, you ought to punish our accusers. For we are accused of being Christians, and to hate what is excellent is unjust." (Ch. 2) "For as some who have been taught by the Master, Christ, not to deny him, give encouragement to others when they are put to the question, so in all probability, those who live wicked lives give occasion to those who, without consideration, take upon them to accuse all the Christians of impiety and wickedness." (Ch. 2)

"To illustrate, isn't it true that among the Greeks all types of men are called philosophers, even though their teachings are quite diverse and many of them simply teach whatever pleases them." (Ch. 7) "Man's coming into existence was not in his own power." (Ch. 10) "Marcion teaches his followers that there is some other God greater than the Creator." (Ch. 26) "Just like many are called philosophers even though they teach the opposite of the other philosophers." (Ch. 26) "I don't think it's inappropriate here to mention how so many of your people, out of fear, worshipped the evil Emperor Antinous as a god even though they knew he was only a man, and a wicked one at that."(Ch. 29) "What kind of things are taught through the prophets from [the person] of God, you can now perceive." (Ch. 37)

"An intelligent man will be able to comprehend [these things] from what has been so largely said already. And we, since the proof of this subject is less needful now, will pass for the present to the proof of those things which are urgent." (Ch. 46) "The nose, by which living creatures breathe, extends from the forehead." (Ch. 55) "All your state possessions are made using these banners as the insignia of your power and government, even though you do so unwittingly." (Ch. 55) "And with this form you consecrate the images of your emperors when they die, and you name them gods by inscription." (Ch. 55)

Index

Will The Real Heretics Please Stand Up

By David W. Bercot

The two works you have just read have given you a sample of early Christianity. Would you like to learn more about the early Christians? If so, we recommend *Will the Real Heretics Please Stand Up*. It's written in a free-flowing readable style, combined with sound scholarship. This 192 page book provides a broad overview of the early Christians—who they were, how they lived, and what they believed. It also explains how the Christianity of that time was lost. Finally, this eye-opening book calls today's church to return to the simple holiness, unfailing love, and patient cross-bearing of the early Christians.

Available at quality Christian bookstores

Or order directly from Scroll Publishing Co., Rt. 19, Box 890, Suite 211, Tyler TX 75706. Simply enclose $6.95, plus $1.00 for shipping and handling, for each copy. Your copy will be shipped to you the same day we receive your request.

The One Who Knows God

By Clement of Alexandria

If you could have sat at the feet of a respected Christian teacher in the second century, what would you have learned? What insights would he have had on the Christian life?

One such teacher was Clement of Alexandria. After his conversion, Clement traveled throughout the ancient world to learn Christianity firsthand from the most respected teachers of his age—men who taught by deeds, not just words. Clement eventually settled in Alexandria, Egypt, where he was made an elder. In recognition of Clement's gift of teaching, the church of Alexandria appointed him as the instructor of new Christians. Some of Clement's written instructions have been preserved through the centuries.

The One Who Knows God is a collection of Clement's godly insights on what it really means to know God. In these writings, Clement discusses prayer, the life of holiness, separation from the world, marriage, wealth, love, women of wisdom, and the secret of tapping into God's power. *The One Who Knows God* will be available at quality Christian bookstores after March 1, 1990. Or it may be ordered after that date directly from Scroll Publishing Co., Rt. 19, Box 890, Suite 211, Tyler, TX 75706. Simply enclose $6.95, plus $1.00 for shipping and handling.

For those who are interested in an in-depth study of early Christianity, Wm. B. Eerdmans Publishing Company has published a set of all the early Christian writings (except for the commentaries of Origen) entitled *The Ante-Nicene Fathers*. It can be obtained from Christian mail order distributors for about $150.00.

Baker Book House has published some of the writings of Ignatius, Polycarp, Justin Martyr, and other early Christian writers in a paperback edition, entitled *The Apostolic Fathers* ($9.95). Macmillan Publishing Co. has also published some of the second century Christian writings in a paperback edition, entitled *Early Christian Fathers* ($10.95). Both of these books can be obtained through most Christian bookstores.